ATLAS
4

Learning-Centered
Communication

David Nunan

Heinle & Heinle Publishers
A Division of International Thomson Publishing, Inc.
Boston, MA 02116, U.S.A.

   The ITP logo is a trademark under license.

The publication of ATLAS was directed by the members of the Heinle & Heinle Global Innovations Publishing Team:

Elizabeth Holthaus, ESL Team Leader
David C. Lee, Editorial Director
John F. McHugh, Market Development Director
Lisa McLaughlin, Production Editor
Nancy Mann, Developmental Editor

Also participating in the publication of the program were:

Publisher: Stanley J. Galek
Assistant Editor: Kenneth Mattsson
Associate Production Editor: Maryellen Eschmann
Manufacturing Coordinator: Mary Beth Hennebury
Series Design: Ligature, Inc.
Page Design and Production Mangement: Rollins Design and Production
Composition and Realia Design: Greg Johnson, Art Directions

Manufactured in the United States of America.

ISBN: 0-8384-4088-6

Heinle & Heinle Publishers is a division of International Thomson Publishing, Inc.

10 9 8 7 6 5 4 3 2 1

Preface

Atlas is a four-level ESL/EFL course for young adults and adults. Its learner-centered, task-based approach motivates learners and helps to create an active, communicative classroom.

Atlas develops the four language skills of listening, speaking, reading, and writing in a systematic and integrated fashion. Each level is designed to cover from 60 to 90 hours of classroom instruction. It can also be adapted for shorter or longer courses; suggestions for doing so are provided in the teacher's extended edition.

Each level of Atlas consists of the following components:

Student's Book:	The student's book contains 12 "core" units and 3 review units. Following the 15 units are "Communication Challenges," which provide extra communicative practice to conclude each unit. Grammar summaries for each unit appear at the end of the book, along with an irregular verb chart.
Teacher's Extended Edition:	The teacher's extended edition contains an introduction to the philosophy of the course, general guidelines for teaching with Atlas, detailed teaching suggestions for each unit, and extension activities. It also includes the tapescript and answer keys for the textbook and the workbook.
Teacher Tape:	The tape contains spoken material for all of the listening activities in the student text.
Workbook:	The workbook provides practice and expansion of the vocabulary, structures, functions, and learning strategies in the student text.
Workbook Tape:	The workbook tape contains spoken material for all of the listening activities in the workbook.
Video:	The video, which contains lively, real-life material, provides reinforcement and expansion of the topics and functions found in the student text.
Assessment Package:	The assessment package will be available in 1995.

FEATURES | BENEFITS

FEATURES	BENEFITS
Unit goals are explicitly stated at the beginning of each unit.	Awareness of goals helps students to focus their learning.
Listening and reading texts are derived from **high-interest, authentic source material.**	Naturalistic/realistic language prepares students for the language they will encounter outside the classroom.
Each unit is built around two **task chains,** sequences of tasks that are linked together in principled ways and in which succeeding tasks are built on those that come before.	Task chains enhance student interest and motivation by providing students with integrated learning experiences.
Units feature explicit focus on **learning strategies.**	Conscious development of a range of learning strategies helps students become more effective learners both in and out of class.
End-of-unit **Self-Check** section encourages students to record and reflect on what they have learned.	Developing personal records of achievement increases student confidence and motivation.

Table of Contents

Language Focus Structures	Learning Strategies	Communication Challenges
- prepositional phrases - modals: *can/could/would/would mind*	- scanning* - selective listening - brainstorming - practicing - cooperating - personalizing	- Simulation: Planning a festival
- short responses - relative adverbials: *where/when/why/how*	- predicting* - making inferences - selective listening - evaluating - scanning - personalizing	- Interview: Rescued!
- present perfect & simple past - emphasis with *it* & *what*	- personalizing* - brainstorming - choosing - making inferences - practicing - lateral thinking	- Lateral thinking: Meeting new people
- *when* & *if* clauses + modal *should/shouldn't* - relative clauses with *whose/who/who is*	- discovering* - selective listening - skimming - brainstorming - evaluating - cooperating	- Discussion: Caring and sharing
- passives: past & perfect forms - reported speech	- classifying* - selective listening - brainstorming - personalizing - making inferences - predicting	- Spot the difference: Wild party
- relative clauses with *that* & *whose* - superlative adjectives with present perfect	- skimming* - role playing - classifying - choosing - evaluating - selective listening	- Information gap: Eco-tour
- two-part verbs + gerunds - indirect questions & requests	- memorizing conversational patterns and expressions* - selective listening - practicing - cooperating - reflecting - lateral thinking	- Simulation: Corporate image

*The asterisked learning strategies are explicitly taught in the unit. The others are used passively.

you're invited . . . to to the movies!   meet me for lunc
what do you do?   why
is my family   neighborhood

Language Focus Structures	Learning Strategies	Communication Challenges
• object + infinitive • past conditional	• brainstorming* • cooperating • personalizing • practicing • selective listening • summarizing	• Group work: A good cause

• *wh-* questions +
  gerund/infinitive
• comparative/superlative +
  gerund/infinitive
	• role playing*
	• selective listening
	• making inferences
	• discriminating
	• predicting
	• top-down reading
		• Information gap: The best person

• future perfect • tag questions	• practicing* • brainstorming • lateral thinking • selective listening • predicting • matching	• Information gap: Leadership
• review of past & perfect tenses • *supposed to*	• selective listening* • personalizing • cooperating • making inferences • skimming • self-evaluation	• Group task: Sequencing information
• complex passives • idioms	• cooperating* • selective listening • matching • personalizing • skimming • reflecting	• Debate: Graffiti
		• Group work: Evaluating others' opinions

*The asterisked learning strategies are explicitly taught in the unit. The others are used passively.

Acknowledgments

Many people were involved in the planning and development of Atlas, and it is impossible for me to mention them all by name. However, special thanks must go to the following:

The reviewers, who helped to shape Atlas:

Lucia de Aragão, Uniao Cultural, São Paulo, **Eric Beatty**, Institut Franco-Américain, Rennes, **Rosamunde Blanck**, City University of New York, Hiroshima, **Richard Berwick**, University of British Columbia, Vancouver, **Jennifer Bixby**, Acton, Massachusetts, **Eric Bray**, YMCA English School, Kyoto, **Vincent Broderick**, Soai College, Osaka, **Chiou-Lan Chern**, Tunghai University, Taichung, **Katy Cox**, Casa Thomas Jefferson, Brasilia, **Richard Evanoff**, Aoyama Gakuin University, Tokyo, **Charles Frederickson, Katherine Harrington**, Associacao Alumni, São Paulo, **Phyllis Herrin de Obregon**, Universidade Autonoma de Querétaro, Querétaro, **James Kahny**, Language Institute of Japan, Tokyo, **Thomas Kanemoto**, Kanda Institute of Foreign Languages, Tokyo, **Maidy Kiji**, Konan Women's University, Kobe, **Richard Klecan**, Miyagi Gakuin, Sendai, **Susan Kobashigawa, Thomas Kral**, United States Information Agency, Washington, D.C., **David Levy**, McGill University, Montreal, **Angela Llanas**, Instituto Anglo-Mexicano, Mexico City, **Thomas Long**, ELS International, Seoul, **David Ludwig**, Crane Publishing Company, Taipei, **Carole McCarthy**, CEGEP ST-Hyacinthe, Quebec, **Jane McElroy**, University of Rio Grande, Tokyo, **John Moore and Aviva Smith**, ECC Foreign Language Institute, Tokyo, **Rebecca Oxford**, University of Alabama, Tuscaloosa, **Margene Petersen**, ELS, Philadelphia, Pennsylvania, **James Riordan and Adelaide Oliveira**, Associacao Cultural, Salvador, **Andrea Safire**, Berkeley, California, **Charles Sandy**, Chubu University Junior College, Nagoya, **Tamara Swenson**, Osaka Jogakuin Junior College, Osaka

The teachers and students in the following institutions, who field-tested early versions of Atlas and provided invaluable comments and suggestions:

AEON, Japan, **Aoyama Gakuin University**, Tokyo, **Associacao Alumni**, São Paulo, **Associacao Cultural**, Salvador, **Associacao Cultural**, Ribeirão Prêto, **AEON**, **Boston University**, Boston, Massachusetts, **Centro Cultural Brasil–Estados Unidos**, Campinas, **Concordia University**, Montreal, **ELS International**, Seoul, **GEOS**, Japan, **Huron University**, Tokyo, **Instituto Anglo-Mexicano**, Mexico City, **Konan Women's University**, Kobe, **LaGuardia Community College**, Long Island City, New York, **Miyagi Gakuin**, Sendai, **Osaka Jogakuin Junior College**, Osaka, **SHOWA Women's University**, Boston, Massachusetts, **Soai College**, Osaka, **Southwest Community College**, Los Angeles, **Tokyo Foreign Language College**, Tokyo, **Universidade Autonoma de Querétaro**, Querétaro, **Waseda University**, Tokyo, **YMCA English School**, Kyoto

Other reviewers, too numerous to mention, helped make this course what it is. Particular thanks must go to Ellen Shaw, who is quite simply the best editor in the business and whose detailed editing and comments strengthened the materials in many different ways. Thanks also to Clarice Lamb, whose unflinching faith in the project helped me maintain my own faith through periods of difficulty and doubt.

I should also like to acknowledge and thank the various International Thomson Publishing and Heinle & Heinle representatives who facilitated field testing and whose personal assistance during visits associated with the development and promotion of Atlas was invaluable. I should like to thank Robert Cullen in Singapore, Carol Chen in Taipei, and Hisae Inami in Tokyo for their particular assistance and support.

Particular thanks are due to my editors at Heinle & Heinle, who helped at all stages in the planning and development of Atlas. Special thanks are due to Charlie Heinle and Stan Galek, for their personal interest and support from the very beginning of the project; to José Wehnes, for his unique marketing philosophy; to Dave Lee, who helped guide the project; to Chris Foley, who helped shape the initial philosophy; to Meg Morris, for her research and data-gathering skills; and to Lisa McLaughlin, for her dedication to ensuring the visual appeal of the book. Most of all, thanks are due to my developmental editor, Nancy Mann, for her professional skills, her quiet good humor, and her happy acceptance of late-night calls.

Celebrations

Warm-Up

Thailand

Unit Goals

In this unit you will:

Give details about special events

"The festival will start in the morning."

Make and respond to invitations and requests

"We would be delighted if you could make it to our wedding."

Brazil

Australia

Hong Kong

1 Group Work Discussion. What do you think the people are celebrating?

2 a Make a list of the things you celebrate and put them into the following categories.

Personal	Public
(things you, your family, and friends celebrate)	*(things other people also celebrate)*
▪ your parents' wedding anniversary	▪ the last day of school
▪ your birthday	▪ New Year's Eve
....	....
....	....

"In my country, people always give gifts for birthdays, weddings, and the birth of a child. And they sometimes bring small gifts, such as flowers or chocolates, when they go to a dinner party."

b Compare your list with another student.

3 Group Work In this unit we will look at the custom of giving gifts. When do people give gifts in your country?

Task Chain 1 Festivals

Celebrations
religious

Task 1

a **GroupWork** Brainstorm. What types of celebrations do societies have? Make a list.

b Look at the pictures on page 9 and draw lines to match the places with their festivals.

Place	Festival
1 Thailand	Dragon Boat Festival
2 Brazil	Water Festival
3 Australia	Carnival
4 Hong Kong	Festival of Arts

Task 2

a 🎧 Listen to the tape. Number the following segments (1 to 4) when you hear them.

.... casual conversation
.... tour guide
.... TV talk show
.... advertisement

b 🎧 Listen again. Look at Task 1b, and circle the names of the places and festivals that you hear.

c 🎧 Listen once more. Which festivals are these people talking about? What do they say about the festivals? Fill in the chart.

NAME	PLACE	FESTIVAL	TYPE/CHARACTERISTICS
Jack			
Paula			
Suriwong			
Nina			

LEARNING STRATEGY

Scanning = searching a text for specific information

Task 3

The writer of the following letter has gotten some of his facts wrong. Scan the brochure and then correct the letter for him.

where you're invited... go to the movies!
is my family
why neighborhood
what do you do?
meet me for lunch

Dragon Boat Festival

The 2,000-year-old Dragon Boat (*Tuan Ng*) Festival commemorates the death in the third century B.C. of Chinese national hero Qu Yuan. Qu Yuan drowned himself in the Mi Lo River to protest the corrupt government. Legend has it that villagers raced their boats towards him in a vain attempt to save his life, striking their paddles on the water, beating drums, and throwing rice dumplings wrapped in bamboo leaves into the river. The paddles and drums were supposed to scare the fish away and stop them from eating Qu Yuan's body.

Today rice dumplings wrapped in bamboo leaves are a traditional festival food, but the real highlight of the festival is the colorful Dragon Boat races. The special boats, which range in length from 38 to 120 feet, have ornately carved and painted dragon heads and tails. Each boat carries a crew of 22 or more paddlers.

Race participants train in earnest for the competition. Sitting two abreast with a steersman at the back and a drummer at the front, the paddlers race to reach the finishing line, urged on by the pounding drums and the roar of the crowd.

The Hong Kong Dragon Boat Festival and International Races take place on a Saturday and Sunday in the middle of June. One hundred and sixty teams (including 32 from overseas) enter the races, which are held off the Tsim Sha Tsui East waterfront.

Dear Sergio,

I've just had the greatest time in Hong Kong at the Dragon Boat Festival, which is held here every June. The festival has been going on for 1,500 years. It's meant to celebrate Chinese Emperor Qu Yuan who drowned while swimming in the Mi Lo River. Apparently some sailors tried to rescue him, but failed. They hit the water with their paddles, beat drums, and threw rice dumplings wrapped in bamboo leaves into the river for him to eat. The races held these days are based on this event that was supposed to have happened all those years ago. There are people and boat racing teams here from twenty different countries. It was a fantastic event, and one that I can thoroughly recommend. I'll write again soon. Next week I'm off to Bangkok.

Sincerely,
Joshua

Task 4

You choose. Do **A** or **B**.

A **Group Work** Think of a festival or special event and describe what you do on that day. Your classmates will guess what festival or event it is.

B Think of the most interesting or exciting holiday you've ever had and describe it to your classmates.

Language Focus 1 Prepositional phrases

1 a Correct the mistakes in the underlined phrases.

b **Pair Work** Can you find any other prepositional phrases? Underline them.

> I lived <u>on Deep Springs</u> <u>during five years</u> and found it really interesting. Each year, there was an arts and crafts festival, beginning <u>in the first day of Fall.</u> The festival was held in an old factory near the edge of town. It was great, because the organizers catered to many different tastes in music, art, and even theater. While there were events during the day, the best performances were <u>in night.</u> People would come to the festival from all over the world. It used to get so crowded that we'd go there <u>in foot,</u> rather than in a car. People traveling through Deep Springs on their way <u>at other destinations</u> would often stop for the festival instead of going on to their intended destination.

PLACE	TIME	EITHER

2 Classify these prepositions according to whether they introduce phrases of place or time.

in	under	on	above	during	over
since	to	into	onto	for	towards

3 a Fill in the blanks with the correct prepositions. Now decide who you think might have made each statement.

Example: During the day I lie in bed, and then ...*at*.. night I go out to work. ..*a security guard*...

1 .... the morning, I get up .... five o'clock, and exercise .... about eight. ....

2 They ran .... me calling me terrible names. ....

3 We were .... the shelter of some trees when the lightning struck. ....

4 I haven't been back there .... they threw me out. ....

5 They've turned the place where I was born .... a tourist attraction. ....

b **Group Work** Compare responses. Who had the most interesting/original choices?

4 **Pair Work** Use these phrases to make statements that are true for you.

a in the morning
b for most of my childhood
c in the place where I was born
d during the summer
e since I was a young kid

"Nothing much ever happens in the place where I was born, which is why I don't live there any more."

"I'd give the tie to my brother for his birthday because it's loud and tasteless—just like him!"

Task 1

a **Pair Work** Discuss with a partner who you would give these gifts to and for what occasion.

b **Group Work** Compare your choices with another pair's.

Task 2

a 🎧 Listen to the first interview and ask the teacher to stop the tape whenever you hear a question. Write the questions below.

....
....
....

b 🎧 Listen again and fill in the chart for all three interviews.

PERSON	FAVORITE GIFT	NEXT BIRTHDAY	OTHER PEOPLE	COST
Mariel				
Natasha				
Rod				

"Well, Natasha is most like me, because she chooses things that people wouldn't buy for themselves—just like me."

c Rank the people from most to least like you in terms of their gift-giving habits (1 to 3).

d **Group Work** Talk about your choices.

Task 3

Group Work Interview two classmates and fill in the chart.

	PERSON 1	PERSON 2
What's the nicest gift that you've received?		
What gift would you most like to receive?		
When do you give gifts?		
How do you choose gifts for others?		
How much do you usually spend?		

Task 4

Pair Work Study the following excerpts from letters and notes. Match each excerpt with its writer.

.... someone planning a surprise party for a friend
.... someone planning a birthday dinner for an elderly relative
.... someone inviting a friend to a party
.... someone inviting a relative to a wedding

a "I hope you can make it."

b "and most of the arrangements have been made. Unfortunately, I haven't been able to contact Mack. Do you think you'll see him at the game on Saturday? Remind him not to say a word, of course."

c "It will only be a small gathering, but John and I would be delighted if you could make it. The ceremony will be in the park, and then we'll go to John's parent's place for the reception."

d "We won't be able to eat too late, of course, but it would be great if you could make it."

Task 5

a Someone invites you to a birthday party, but you don't want to go. What are you most likely to do? Rank these options from most to least likely (1 to 5 or 6).

.... change the topic
.... say you are already busy
.... end the conversation without saying "yes" or "no."
.... remain silent
.... say you don't want to go
.... other (specify): ....

b **Pair Work** Compare your choices with another student's.

Language Focus 2 Modals: can/could/would/would mind

1 🎧 **Pair Work** Listen. Then practice the conversation.

A: Hello, Tomoko?
B: Oh, hi Jim.
A: I'm calling to see if you can come to my party on Saturday night.
B: I can't, sorry. I'm having dinner with a friend.
A: Would you be able to come later?
B: Well, I guess I could come around eleven. Would you mind if I brought my friend?
A: No, not at all. See you then.

2 a **Pair Work** Have a conversation, using these functions.

A: (Call up your partner.)
B: (Answer the phone.)
A: (Invite your friend to a birthday party/dinner/the movies.)
B: (Say no and give an excuse.)
A: (Suggest an alternative.)
B: (Accept or decline the alternative.)

b **Pair Work** Now change roles and have the conversation again.

3 Rank these requests from least formal to most formal (1 to 4).

.... I wonder if you'd mind copying this report for me?
.... Could you invite Mike to the party?
.... Would you mind if I brought Marco to your party?
.... Can you pass the ketchup?

4 a Which of these phrases would you use for the following situations?

1 "I wonder if you'd mind"
2 "Could you"
3 "Would you mind"
4 "Can you"

.... You want your younger brother/sister to hand you a book.
.... You want your teacher to tell you your exam results.
.... You want your best friend to pick up the tickets for a show.
.... You want a friend to write down a phone number for you.
.... You want a stranger to tell you the time.

b **Pair Work** Compare your responses with another student's response.

c **Pair Work** Take turns role playing these situations.

Self-Check

COMMUNICATION CHALLENGE

PairWork Look at Challenge 1 on page 111.

1 Write down five new words you learned in this unit.

....

2 Write sentences using three of these new words.

....

....

....

3 Write three new sentences or questions you learned.

....

....

....

4 a

WHAT WOULD YOU SAY?

Your best friend invites you to his/her birthday party, but you can't make it.

You say: ....

You want someone to get you a book from the library.

You say: ....

You are telling friends about a festival you went to.

You say: ....

b GroupWork Brainstorm ways to practice this language out of class. Imagine you are visiting an English-speaking country. Where/When might you need this language?

5 Out of Class Find out about a festival in your country. See if you can find out some unusual facts about the event. Bring the information to class and be prepared to talk about it.

6 Vocabulary check. Check [√] the words you know.

Adjectives/Adverbs			Nouns		Verbs		Prepositions
☐ always	☐ interesting	☐ unfortunately	☐ advertisement	☐ gift	☐ celebrate	☐ remain	☐ above
☐ busy	☐ loud	☐ usually	☐ alternative	☐ habit	☐ choose	☐ rescue	☐ during
☐ casual	☐ personal	☐ vain	☐ celebration	☐ hero	☐ commemorate	☐ respond	☐ for
☐ colorful	☐ public		☐ ceremony	☐ invitation	☐ drown	☐ scan	☐ in
☐ corrupt	☐ silent		☐ competition	☐ news broadcast	☐ get up		☐ into
☐ delighted	☐ sometimes		☐ conversation	☐ participant	☐ invite	**Modal Verbs**	☐ on
☐ elderly	☐ special		☐ custom	☐ program	☐ lend	☐ can	☐ onto
☐ exciting	☐ sports		☐ details	☐ reception	☐ practice	☐ could	☐ over
☐ fantastic	☐ tasteless		☐ excuse	☐ request	☐ protest	☐ would	☐ since
☐ gift-giving	☐ traditional		☐ festival	☐ talk show	☐ race	☐ would mind	☐ to
							☐ towards

2 Believe It or Not

Warm-Up

Picture 1

Picture 2

Picture 3

Picture 4

Unit Goals

In this unit you will:

Express degrees of belief and disbelief

"I find that hard to believe."

Give details about events

"The place where the ship went down was just off the coast."

1 a Match the pictures with the statements in Task 1b. Write the number of the picture in the blank at the left.

b How believable do you find these statements? Circle a number.

PICTURE NUMBER	STATEMENT	COMPLETELY BELIEVABLE				COMPLETELY UNBELIEVABLE
....	"My brother and I can tell what each other is thinking—we are telepathic."	1	2	3	4	5
....	"I saw a ghost last year."	1	2	3	4	5
....	"I once experienced astral travel—I actually left my body for several minutes."	1	2	3	4	5
....	"The horoscope in the newspaper last week predicted everything that happened to me this week."	1	2	3	4	5

2 **Group Work** Compare your responses with three or four other students.

Task Chain 1 Stranger than fiction

Task 1

a Check [√] the words you know.

☐ weird	☐ happen	☐ relaxing
☐ junk food	☐ strange	☐ wrong
☐ uncomfortable	☐ ignore	☐ elderly
☐ compulsion	☐ lying	☐ knocked
☐ telepathy	☐ thoughts	☐ mental
☐ messages	☐ rubbish	☐ concentrate
☐ travel	☐ crazy	

b **GroupWork** Discussion. Which are the most familiar and least familiar words in the list?

"For me, the least familiar words are *compulsion* and *concentrate*. The most familiar are *messages* and *travel.*"

Task 2

a 🎧 Listen to the conversation. You will hear about two unusual events. What are the events? Why are they unusual?

EVENT	WHY IS IT UNUSUAL?		
1			
2			

b 🎧 Compare your responses with another student's responses and then listen again to check your answers.

c 🎧 Listen once more. Who believes in telepathy, doesn't believe, isn't sure? Put a check [√] in the correct column.

	Believes	*Not sure*	*Doesn't believe*
Pete	☐	☐	☐
Mark	☐	☐	☐
Gina	☐	☐	☐

Task 3

a Skim the following story. What do you think it is about? Check [√] one box.

☐ telepathy   ☐ astral travel   ☐ coincidence

Lucien felt that Joan and Bill had an understanding on some deep level that people rarely achieve, something on a <u>psychic level</u> that you could actually feel. Sitting in the living room of their small apartment, he watched them play their favorite game. They sat at opposite ends of the room, and each one took a sheet of paper and divided it into nine squares, and drew a picture in each of the squares, and when they had finished they compared the drawings and there was an <u>uncanny correlation</u>—they had both drawn a scorpion, and they had both drawn a bottle, and they had both drawn a dog. About half the drawings were the same. To Lucien, the degree of telepathic communication was <u>spooky</u>.

From *Literary Outlaw: The Life and Times of William S. Burroughs*, by T. Morgan.

b Scan the story and decide which of the underlined words and phrases mean:

mysterious and a little frightening ....
extraordinary similarity ....
spiritual dimension ....

c Do you think that the story is unusual? Do you think that the event could simply have been a coincidence?

Task 4

a **Pair Work** Think of a number between 1 and 10. Write it on a piece of paper, but don't let your partner see. Concentrate on the number for ten seconds. Your partner will try to guess the number and write it on a piece of paper. Compare numbers. Repeat this several times. How often were you successful?

b **Pair Work** Now change roles and do the task again.

c **Group Work** Compare results with other class members.

Task 5

Group Work Discussion.

a Have you ever had an unusual experience similar to those discussed in Task 2?

b Do you know anybody else who has had experiences like these?

c Can you think of explanations other than telepathy to account for the events?

Language Focus 1 Short responses

1 **Pair Work** Match the questions and responses and then practice them with your partner.

Questions

a Are you still reading that awful horoscope column in the newspaper?

b Did you know that I saw a ghost once when I was a kid?

c Have you seen the guy on TV who can bend spoons by looking at them?

Responses

.... I find that hard to believe.

.... No, not yet.

.... Not since it said I'd win a million dollars.

2 a Underline the response that you would give to these questions.

1 Do you believe in telepathy?
  a) I used to.
  b) Not since I was a child.
  c) No, it's all in your head.

2 Have you ever seen a ghost?
  a) Only once.
  b) No, not yet.
  c) No, but I expect to soon.

3 Are you still practicing telepathy?
  a) Only occasionally.
  b) I never did.
  c) Not recently.

4 Are you superstitious?
  a) Only occasionally.
  b) Yes, every time I see my former teacher.
  c) Not unless I'm waiting for my exam results.

b **Pair Work** Now practice the questions and responses with a partner.

3 a Think of questions or statements for these responses.

1 ....
I find that hard to believe.

2 ....
You're kidding.

3 ....
Only on the weekend.

4 ....
No, not yet.

b **Pair Work** Now practice them with a partner.

Task 1

a **Group Work** Put these pictures in order to make a story.

Picture ....

Picture ....

Picture ....

Picture ....

Picture ....

LEARNING STRATEGY

Predicting = saying what you think will happen.

b Now tell the story using some of these words.

fell overboard	survived
rough conditions	pulled from water
taken ashore	reunited with wife

Task 2

a Read the following newspaper story and see if you can find two facts and one opinion. Underline the facts and circle the opinion.

HEADLINE:

....

by Rebecca Hill

Champion yachtsman Pete Estrada came ashore at San Diego yesterday after being rescued from a harrowing five hours in the open ocean. Supposedly one of the best sailors in the sport, Estrada survived in freezing conditions after being swept from his yacht during a race. The 49-year-old sailor, who is lucky to be alive, was found by a tanker after his cries for help were heard. The tanker shielded Estrada while another yacht, the Victory, moved in, pulled him from the water, and treated him for shock. "They wrapped me in dry wool blankets and one of the guys jumped into the bunk with me and hung on to me, using his body temperature to warm me up," Estrada recounted.

By the time they reached land, Estrada had recovered sufficiently from his ordeal to help the crew moor the boat. However, at the press conference he seemed rather embarrassed by the attention.

The tanker captain who helped rescue Estrada said he hoped to catch up with the sailor in less dramatic circumstances. "He's an extremely lucky man," he said. "The next time I'm in San Diego I may call in to the Yacht Club to buy him a drink."

Estrada has been sailing since he was seven years old and ocean racing since the age of nineteen. But he confessed that after five hours alone in the sea, this was his last voyage.

b **Group Work** Discussion. Compare your responses with 3 or 4 other students' responses. Were there any words or phrases that helped you to decide what was opinion?

c 🎧 Listen and note the similarities and differences between the newspaper report and the broadcast.

SIMILARITIES	DIFFERENCES

d What might be some reasons for the differences?

Task 3

a **Group Work** Discussion. What is the most dramatic experience you have ever had? Describe it to the other students in the group.

b Decide on the most dramatic or interesting story.

c Have one group member tell that story to the class.

Language Focus 2 Relative adverbials: where/when/why/how

"I don't really understand how it happened."

Do you know the rule?

Fill in the chart using the words provided. The first one has been done for you.

how	in	manner
on	when	reason
for	why	during
time		

Preposition + which	Replaced by	Refers to
at, in, to, from	where	place
....	....	....
....	....	....
....	....	....

"Three a.m. was when they told Estrada's wife he was missing."

1 a Draw a line between the two parts of the sentences and join them with one of these words:

when   where   why   how

1 I don't really understand   .... it came looking for me.
2 The place   .... I saw the lights of a tanker coming towards me.
3 I saw the boat's lights   .... they didn't see me was because of the huge waves.
4 The reason   .... it happened was about 50 kilometers from shore.
5 It was around 5 a.m.   ...*why*.. it happened, but it did.

b **Pair Work** Practice the statements. *Student A:* Say the first part of the statement. *Student B:* Complete it.

2 Replace the underlined phrases with one of these words:

when   where   why   how

Example: <u>The way in which</u> the rescue happened was miraculous.
        How the rescue happened was miraculous.

a The spot <u>at which</u> the accident happened was extremely remote.
....

b No one can understand <u>the way in which</u> the accident happened.
....

c Winter is the season <u>during which</u> most boating fatalities occur.
....

d The reports never explained <u>the reason for which</u> the tanker was moving towards the coast. ....

e <u>The manner in which</u> Estrada survived amazed everyone.
....

3 **Group Work** Think of something that happened to you recently. Tell the group when, where, how, and why the incident happened.

Self-Check

GroupWork Student A: Look at page 112. Student B: Look at page 114. Student C: Look at page 116.

1 Write down five new words you learned in this unit.

....

2 Write sentences using three of these new words.

....

....

....

3 Write three new sentences or questions you learned.

....

....

....

4 a

WHAT WOULD YOU SAY?

Someone tells you that they once saw a ghost.

You say: ....

Someone asks you about the most dramatic thing that ever happened to you.

You say: ....

b **GroupWork** Brainstorm ways to practice this language out of class. Imagine you are visiting an English-speaking country. Where/When might you need this language?

5 **Out of Class** Interview friends, family, and acquaintances and find somebody who has had a strange experience. Report the story to the class. Who has the most interesting, unusual, or hard-to-believe story?

6 Vocabulary check. Check [√] the words you know.

Adjectives/Adverbs

☐ believable	☐ mental	☐ spooky
☐ confused	☐ mysterious	☐ superstitious
☐ crazy	☐ occasionally	☐ telepathic
☐ dramatic	☐ psychic	☐ unbelievable
☐ freezing	☐ remote	☐ uncanny
☐ frightening	☐ rescued	☐ weird
☐ lucky	☐ spiritual	

Nouns

☐ astral travel	☐ disbelief	☐ press
☐ belief	☐ explanation	conference
☐ champion	☐ fiction	☐ shock
☐ coincidence	☐ ghost	☐ similarity
☐ compulsion	☐ horoscope	☐ voyage
☐ correlation	☐ junk food	☐ yacht

Verbs

☐ account	☐ kid	☐ survive
☐ concentrate	☐ predict	
☐ interview	☐ shield	

3 Origins

Warm-Up

Canada

United States

Unit Goals

In this unit you will:

Emphasize information

"What makes my country special is the mix of nationalities."

"It's the mix of nationalities that makes my country special."

Talk about past events

"I went to Korea again last summer. I've been there twice now."

Japan

Brazil

Taiwan

France

"I'd like to live in Thailand. It has a rich culture, great food, and wonderful people."

1 a Group Work Brainstorm. Which of the countries pictured could these statements be about? (Note: There is no single correct answer for this task.)

1 What makes my country special is the fact that it is very safe, there is very little unemployment, and salaries are good.

2 What makes my country special is the sense of excitement. There's a lot of energy, and it affects everyone.

3 What makes my country special is the fact that our population is made up of people from many different parts of the world.

4 That's very simple. What makes my country special is the culture, the food, and the wine.

b Can you think of any other countries that match these statements?

2 a Would you like to live in another country for a while? Make a list of three countries you would like to live in and give reasons.

b Pair Work Share your list with another student.

Task 1

Group Work How much do you know about U.S. history? Take this quiz to find out. Try to put these events in chronological order by numbering them 1 to 5.

.... Large numbers of Spanish-speaking people arrived from Mexico and the West Indies.

.... The English colonies rebelled against England in the Revolutionary War.

.... Spanish settlers arrived in Florida and Mexico.

.... Many British, French, Dutch, Germans, and Swedish people immigrated to the U.S.

.... Millions of immigrants arrived from Europe and Asia.

LEARNING STRATEGY

Personalizing = sharing your own opinions, feelings, and ideas about a subject.

Task 2

Now check your answers to Task 1 by reading the following encyclopedia entry.

Immigration in the United States

First settled by "Indian" groups who migrated from Asia across the Bering land bridge over 25,000 years ago, the country was explored by the Norse (9th century), and by the Spanish (16th century) who settled in Florida and Mexico. In the 17th century there were settlements by the British, French, Dutch, Germans, and Swedish. Many Africans were introduced as slaves to work on the plantations. In the following century, British control grew throughout the area. A revolt of the English-speaking colonies in the War of Independence (1775-83) led to the creation of the United States of America.

In the 19th century millions of immigrants arrived from Europe and Asia, many of them refugees, leading to the description of the U.S.A. as a "melting pot" of nations. More recently, large numbers of Spanish-speaking people have arrived mainly from Central and South America.

Adapted from *Cambridge Encyclopedia*

"I think that most people emigrate for economic reasons."

Task 3

a Group Work Brainstorm. Can you think of reasons why people emigrate?

you're invited . . . go to the movies! meet me for lunch
what do you do?
why
is my family neighborhood

b Think of one or two possible reasons for the following facts.

FACT	REASON(S)
In the 19th century, many people moved from Ireland to the U.S.	
Many people emigrated from Europe to Canada and the U.S. between 1946-56.	
Many people left the former Soviet Union in the 1920s.	
Many people left Hong Kong in the early 1990s.	
There was an increase in immigration to Australia in the 1950s and 60s.	
Many people left Lebanon during the 1980s.	

c Compare your reasons with another group.

Task 4

REASON	COUNTRY
1	
2	
3	
4	
5	

a 🎧 Listen to the lecture and list the reasons why people emigrate.

b 🎧 Listen again. What countries are mentioned in connection with each reason?

c Compare the responses you gave in Task 3 with the information in the lecture you just heard.

Task 5

You choose: Do **A** or **B**.

A Make notes about the development of your own country. Answer questions such as:
- When did the population grow most quickly?
- Where did the people come from?
- Why did people emigrate from/immigrate to your country?

Group Work Tell your classmates about the development of your country.

B The following is some information about the development of Canada. Based on the information, write a paragraph about the settlement of Canada.

IMMIGRATION TO CANADA						
Thousands of Years Ago	Late 1700s	1763	Late 1800s	1945–early 1960s	1975–1985	1980s–early 1990s
Inuits, Indians	Scottish settlers	Quebec became part of Canada; 65,0000 French were living there	Other European immigrants arrived	After World War II, the greatest wave of immigration	113,000 refugees from Cambodia, Laos, Vietnam	Many immigrants from Hong Kong

Language Focus 1 — Present perfect & simple past

1 🎧 **PairWork** Listen. Then practice the conversation.

A: Why did you decide to go to Japan?
B: I've always been fascinated by Japanese culture and I've read a lot about the country and its people, and I wanted to see it for myself.
A: And what did you think?
B: Well, it was the most incredible experience I've ever had.

2 **PairWork** Complete these statements using the present perfect (*have lived*) for one statement and the simple past tense (*lived*) for the other statement.

Example: Lilly and Jo are fluent in Portuguese, even though they . . .

1 *have never lived* (never live) in a Portuguese-speaking country.
2 *didn't learn* (not learn) it until they were in their twenties.

a Tom made his first visit to Japan last year.

1 He .... (enjoy) it so much that he plans to return next year.
2 He .... (show) us his slide collection five times since his return.

b It was Sylvia's mother's third marriage.

1 She .... (fall) in love with her third husband at first sight.
2 She .... (not be) so happy since her second husband left.

c Kanya is my best friend, although I . . .

1 .... (not see) her for weeks.
2 .... (not like) her very much when I first met her.

d They finally settled in Australia two years ago.

1 They .... (regret) the decision ever since they moved.
2 They originally .... (go) there for a vacation.

3 Fill in the blanks with an appropriate form of the verb in parentheses.

a We .... (be) at the party since it started.

b We .... (miss) the concert because we didn't get tickets.

c Since that wild party last week, I .... (decide) I'm not the party type.

d I .... (not see) you at Paul's place last week.

e I .... (not go) to a party since my brother's birthday.

Do you know the rule?

Match the uses of the simple past and present perfect with the examples by writing a letter under "example." Indicate which tense, simple past (SP) or present perfect (PP) is being referred to by writing SP or PP under "Tense."

Uses	Example	Tense
1 A state continuing from past to present.	....	....
2 Completed events at a definite time in the past.	....	....
3 Habits or recurring events in a period leading to the present.	....	....

Examples:
a I've been to ten parties in the last month.
b She didn't come to the party because she was sick.
c We've been here for hours.

"Living in another country is really exciting because it gives you an opportunity to learn about another culture."

Task 1

a **Group Work** Brainstorm. Make a list of the good things and the bad things about living in another country.

Good Things

....

....

....

Bad Things

....

....

....

b **Group Work** Now take turns making statements following the model.

Task 2

a 🎧 Listen. You will hear Dave, Anne, and Denise talking about what it's like to live in another country. None of them live in the country where they were born. Make a note of the places you hear.

Dave

Denise

Anne

FACT SHEET

- One of the people living in Australia was born in Britain.
- Denise was born in Australia.
- One of the people living in Australia is from Canada

b 🎧 **Group Work** Listen again. Where were these three people born? Where are they living now? Use the information on the tape and the fact sheet at left to fill in the chart.

NAME	WHERE FROM	WHERE LIVING NOW
Anne		
Denise		
Dave		

c **Group Work** Discussion. What does each person say about "culture"?

NAME	TOPIC	COMMENT
Anne	British culture	
Denise	California culture	
Dave	Popular culture	

d 🎧 Listen to the tape again to check your answers.

Task 3

The following excerpts are from letters written by Anne, Denise, and Dave to friends and family back home not long after they began living in their new country. Who wrote which letter?

Excerpts   *Written by*

I had dinner with my new boss last night. It was interesting, although rather confusing. The conversation was all about movies I'd never seen, writers I'd never read, and singers I'd never heard of.   ....

Physically the country is about the same size, but in every other respect, the differences are simply overwhelming. There are twice as many people in this state than in our whole country.   ....

I've had an interesting time since I arrived. I was invited to my first party on Saturday night, and it was great fun, although I spent the entire evening telling my story over and over, which got a bit frustrating.   ....

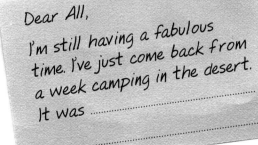

Dear All,
I'm still having a fabulous time. I've just come back from a week camping in the desert. It was ....
....

Task 4

a Pick a country and write an imaginary letter to friends at home. Don't mention the country.

b **Pair Work** Exchange letters and try and guess the country your partner wrote about.

Task 5

You choose: Do **A** or **B**.

A **Pair Work** Make a list of the things that visitors would say about *your* country.

B Make a list of the things that give your country a sense of identity (famous people, significant events in history, etc.).

"Believe it or not, the thing that gives my country a sense of identity is the fact that it's made up of people from all over the world."

Language Focus 2 Emphasis with *it* & *what*

1 🎧 Pair Work Listen. Then practice the conversation using information that is true for you.

A: What makes Canada special for you, Dave?

B: I guess it's the tolerance of the people that makes the place special for me. What also makes it special is the mix of nationalities. We have people here from all over the world. What about you?

A: Well, what makes Australia special is that it's at the end of the earth, so it's still relatively innocent. I guess it's also the mix of people from all over the world. I guess we're a bit like Canada from that perspective.

2 Rewrite these statements. Begin with *what* or *it's*.

Example: It's the lack of unemployment that makes my country special.

What *makes my country special is the lack of unemployment.*

a What makes my country special is the fact that it is very safe.

It's ....

b It's the sense of excitement that makes my country interesting.

What ....

c What makes my country special is the political freedom.

It's ....

d It's the culture, the food, and the wine that make my country unique.

What ....

e What makes my country important is the fact that I was born there!

It's ....

A What I hate about my school is the amount of traveling to get there.

B It's the traveling to get there that Yumi hates about her school.

3 a Pair Work Say what you . . .

like . . .   about your   . . . country
dislike   school
love   friends
admire   etc.

b Report what your partner says to another pair.

Self-Check

COMMUNICATION CHALLENGE

Pair Work Look at Challenge 3 on page 112.

1 Write down five new words you learned in this unit.

....

2 Write sentences using three of these new words.

....
....
....

3 Write three new sentences or questions you learned.

....
....
....

4 a

WHAT WOULD YOU SAY?

Someone asks you what makes your country special.

You say: ....

You want to know what makes a friend's hometown special.

You say: ....

Someone asks you what places you've visited.

You say: ....

b Group Work Brainstorm ways to practice this language out of class. Imagine you are visiting an English-speaking country. Where/When might you need this language?

5 Out of Class Talk to three people who have immigrated to your country from another country or who have spent time living in another country. Ask them about their experiences and report back to the class.

6 Vocabulary check. Check [√] the words you know.

Adjectives/Adverbs			Nouns			Verbs		
☐ confusing	☐ overwhelming	☐ safe	☐ consulate	☐ immigrant	☐ salary	☐ emigrate	☐ immigrate	☐ regret
☐ crazy	☐ political	☐ simple	☐ creation	☐ immigration	☐ settlement	☐ emphasize	☐ introduce	
☐ frustrating	☐ practical	☐ unique	☐ culture	☐ mix	☐ slave	☐ explore	☐ personalize	
☐ incredible	☐ relatively		☐ encyclopedia	☐ perspective	☐ tolerance			
☐ innocent	☐ rich		☐ history	☐ population	☐ unemployment			
			☐ identity	☐ revolt				

4 Good Advice

Warm-Up

Unit Goals

In this unit you will:

Ask for and give advice

"If you stay up late at night, you should take a nap during the day."

"What should I do when I can't get to sleep at night?"

Express preferences

"I prefer people who are neat."

"I dislike people whose friends stay up talking half the night."

1 a Look at the pictures and make a list of the habits you see.

b Group Work Brainstorm. Make a list of group members' good and bad habits.

NAME	GOOD HABITS	BAD HABITS

c Group Work Compare them with another group. Do your good habits seem better than those of the other group? Do their bad habits seem worse than yours?

d Group Work Discussion. What are habits? Why do we have habits?

2 Group Work Listen and discuss. What habit is the speaker talking about? Do you think the habit is normal or rather unusual? Why?

Task 1

Group Work Quiz. How do you feel about sleep? Decide whether the statements below are true or false.

Sleep Quiz	True	False
a. Sleeping during the day is bad for you.	....	....
b. Adults do not need more than six hours' sleep.	....	....
c. Jogging during the day will help you sleep better at night.	....	....
d. Eating a large evening meal can help you sleep.	....	....
e. People who smoke are heavier sleepers than non-smokers.	....	....
f. Going to bed at the same time every night helps us sleep better.	....	....
g. Firm mattresses provide better rest than soft ones.	....	....
h. Going to bed without eating can cause sleeplessness.	....	....

Task 2

"I heard that counting sheep was supposed to help."

a **Group Work** Brainstorm suggestions for helping someone who has trouble sleeping.

b 🎧 You will hear someone getting advice about her sleep problems. Listen and check [√] the things that are causing her difficulty.

	YES	NO	NOT SURE	ADVICE
Worry about work				
Soft mattress				
Going to bed at irregular hours				
Lack of exercise				
Eating a large meal				
Being a smoker				
Drinking coffee				

c 🎧 Listen again. In the last column make a note of any advice that is given.

d 🎧 **Group Work** Which of the true/false items in Task 1 are mentioned in the conversation? Listen once more and check your group's answers to Task 1.

"Both the conversation and the article mention keeping regular hours. The article talks about sleeping on a good bed."

Task 3

a Read the following article and underline the information that was discussed in the conversation in Task 2. Make a list of the new information.

b **Pair Work** Compare your responses with another student.

You *Can* Get a Good Night's Rest!

Nothing is more essential to a good day than a good night's sleep. But on any given night, one in three people has difficulty sleeping and most of us get less sleep than we need. Increasing your comfort while sleeping can be important in helping you get a good night's rest. According to Andrea Herman, director of the Better Sleep Council, "We sometimes sacrifice sleep because of our busy lifestyles. That makes the sleep we do get even more important." Herman suggests you do the following to improve the quality of your sleep.

■ **Keep regular hours.** Try to get up at the same time every morning regardless of how much or how little sleep you've had.

■ **Exercise regularly.** Taking a 30-minute walk, jogging, or swimming three or four times a week will help you sleep better and deeper.

■ **Cut down on caffeine.** This drug, found in coffee, cola, and tea can interfere with sleep. "Drink your last cup of coffee no later than six to eight hours before your usual bedtime," says Herman.

■ **Sleep on a good bed.** "It's difficult to get a good night's rest on a bed that's too small, too hard, or too soft."

■ **Don't smoke.** Studies have found that heavy smokers awaken more times during the night and spend less time in deep sleep than non-smokers.

■ **Go for quality, not quantity.** Six hours of deep, solid sleep will make you feel more rested than eight hours of light, interrupted sleep.

■ **Set aside a "worry" or planning time early in the evening.** To keep from rehearsing your plans or problems while your head's on the pillow, make a list of things to do and of your concerns before you go to bed.

■ **Don't go to bed stuffed or starved.** Heavy, high-fat meals may make you feel drowsy at first, but they can keep you tossing and turning all night. Likewise, your grumbling stomach may prevent deep sleep if you go to bed hungry.

■ **Develop a sleep ritual.** Children often benefit from repeating a calming sleep ritual. Adults also can benefit from a ritual—doing easy stretches, reading a book, taking a warm bath, or listening to music.

Source: Adapted from *Vitality*, August 1994

Task 4

a Survey. Complete the following survey on sleep habits.

	Always	Often	Hardly ever	Never
1 I go to bed at the same time every night.	....	....	....	....
2 I am asleep by 10:30 P.M.	....	....	....	....
3 I am still up at 1 A.M.	....	....	....	....
4 I find it difficult to get to sleep.	....	....	....	....
5 I lie awake worrying about things.	....	....	....	....
6 I take a nap during the day.	....	....	....	....
7 I sleep for more than eight hours.	....	....	....	....

b **Group Work** Now interview two other students.

c **Group Work** Discussion. Which members of the class get the most sleep? The least? Why?

Language Focus 1 *When* and *if* clauses + modal *should/shouldn't*

1 🎧 **Pair Work** Listen to the conversation. Then practice it with a partner.

A: My sister and her husband are coming to visit this weekend.
B: Oh, that's great!
A: Well, it's good and bad. She's very messy, and he's an insomniac.
B: A *what?*
A: An insomniac—someone who has trouble sleeping. He spends most of the night watching TV and keeping everyone else awake.
B: Oh, no.
A: What should I do if she leaves her stuff all over the place?
B: If she leaves her clothes all over the place, you should put them in a bag and send them to the most expensive cleaner in town.
A: What a great idea! And what should I do when her husband keeps us all awake?
B: When you go to bed, take the TV remote control with you.
A: What a great idea!

Do you know the rule?

Complete the following statements by circling the correct alternative.

We use *when* in talking about events that *are going to / might* happen.

We use *if* in talking about events that *are going to / might* happen.

2 **Pair Work** Complete these sentences using *if* or *when*. Then practice making statements and responding to them.

Example:
You win a lot of money. → If you win a lot of money, you should always give some to charity. It brings good luck.

a In a restaurant, you find yourself sitting next to someone whose smoking bothers you.
b You get a low grade on an exam.
c You meet someone for the first time.
d Someone you know well gets married.
e Someone you know well has an accident.

LEARNING STRATEGY

Discovering = finding patterns in language.

3 **Pair Work** What advice would you give to someone . . .

a who has trouble getting to sleep at night?
b whose roommate stays up until very late listening to loud music?
c whose partner snores in their sleep?
d who has trouble getting up in the morning?

4 a **Group Work** Make a list of five or six things you would like advice on. Now circulate and take turns with other students asking for advice.

b **Group Work** Discussion. Who had the most interesting/unusual request for advice? Who had the most creative/unusual advice to give?

"Before you go to bed, you should take a bubble bath."

"I'm always interrupting others in conversation. This is a really annoying habit that I'd like to change."

Task 1

a **Group Work** Discussion. Have you ever tried to quit a bad habit? Do you know anyone else who has? What methods did you/they use? Were the methods successful? Why or why not?

b **Pair Work** Study the following statements and decide how each person gave up their bad habit. Write the number of the method in the blank.

1 support groups   3 physician's advice   5 cold turkey
2 hypnosis   4 self-help approaches

.... "I tried quitting by myself, but it didn't work. I finally went to see our family doctor."

.... "I bought a book and a tape, and managed to cure myself."

.... "Every Tuesday and Thursday, I went over to our local community center and met with five or six other people who were also trying to quit. We'd talk and give each other help and advice."

.... "It worked the very first time. I had to lie down and close my eyes, relax, and just listen to the therapist. I never had the urge to raid the cookie jar again."

.... "I just got up one morning and said to myself, 'That's it!' I stopped completely, just like that. It's the only way to do it."

c Skim the magazine article. Which of these types of support are referred to in the article? Write yes or no in the first column of the chart on page 38.

Kick the Habit

There are numerous ways of giving up bad habits, although not all are equally effective for all habits and all people. The secret of successfully ridding oneself of a bad habit is to match the method, the habit, and one's own personality. Going cold turkey might be fine for someone with an iron will and intense motivation, but not for the person who thinks that success should come in small, achievable steps. Hypnosis might work for someone who wants to quit smoking, or who has an eating disorder, but is probably inappropriate for someone who wants to stop biting their nails. Type of habit and personality will also determine the amount of support that someone will need. Some people are readily able to take advantage of the various self-help options available, while others will need the assistance of support groups in order to kick their habit successfully.

METHOD	REFERRED TO? (YES OR NO)	HABITS	ADVANTAGES	DISADVANTAGES
support groups				
hypnosis				
physician advice				
self-help approaches				
cold turkey				

d Group Work Brainstorm. What habits do you think each method is suited to? Fill in the second column in the chart.

e Group Work What are some advantages and disadvantages of the different methods? Complete the chart, then compare with another group.

Task 2

a 🎧 Listen to the radio call-in show. People are asking for advice on how to kick a habit or how to help someone else to kick a bad habit. In the chart, fill in the habit and the people's unsuccessful methods of quitting.

b 🎧 Listen again and write the suggestions in the chart.

PERSON	HABIT	UNSUCCESSFUL METHOD	SUGGESTION
Camilla			
Tom			
Melissa			

A I want to quit smoking. What should I do?

B Why don't you go cold turkey? That worked for me.

c 🎧 Pair Work Check your responses with another student.

d Group Work Do you think that these suggestions are good ones? Can you think of better suggestions?

Task 3

You choose: Do **A** or **B**.

A Look at the bad habit you listed in Task 1. Ask your partner for advice on how to kick the habit.

B Make a list of habits family members or friends have that annoy you.

Pair Work Think of ways to encourage the people to quit their bad habits. Write them down.

Group Work Discuss your solutions with another pair.

"My friend David is a workaholic. I think he needs to take a vacation every year."

Language Focus 2 Relative clauses with *whose/who/who is*

1 🎧 Listen to the conversation between Mitch and Lisa and complete these statements.

a Lisa likes people who ....

b Lisa doesn't like people whose ....

c Lisa would like to live with someone who's ....

d Mitch likes people whose ....

e Mitch doesn't like people who ....

Who would you like to share a house/apartment with?

	You			Your Partner		
	Y	N	D	Y	N	D
someone who smokes	☐	☐	☐	☐	☐	☐
someone who's a messy cook	☐	☐	☐	☐	☐	☐
someone whose parties go on all night	☐	☐	☐	☐	☐	☐
someone who plays classical music	☐	☐	☐	☐	☐	☐
someone whose relatives are always visiting	☐	☐	☐	☐	☐	☐
someone who's extremely neat	☐	☐	☐	☐	☐	☐
someone who stays home a lot	☐	☐	☐	☐	☐	☐
someone who gets up very early	☐	☐	☐	☐	☐	☐
someone whose boss calls all the time	☐	☐	☐	☐	☐	☐
....	☐	☐	☐	☐	☐	☐
....	☐	☐	☐	☐	☐	☐

2 a Complete the survey at left by checking the appropriate box [√] in column 1.

Key: Y = yes
N = no
D = don't care

b **Pair Work** Now add two items to the list, and then survey a partner on the entire list.

c **Pair Work** Now tell someone else about your partner's preferences.

A "Shelly, would you like to live with someone who goes out a lot?"

B "I don't care."

A (to C) "Shelly doesn't care if she lives with someone who goes out a lot."

Do you know the rule?

Group Work Discussion. When do we use who's and whose?

3 Combine these sentences using *who, who's,* or *whose* and practice them.

a We met some friends at a café. They invited us to a late night party.

b We met some students at the party. Their roommate is moving out.

c I like certain people. Particularly those who are considerate of others.

d I am bored by certain people. Particularly those with limited interests.

e I can't stand certain people. Particularly when they interrupt all the time.

Self-Check

COMMUNICATION CHALLENGE

Look at Challenge 4 on page 113.

1 Write down five new words you learned in this unit.

....

2 Write sentences using three of these new words.

....

....

....

3 Write three new sentences or questions you learned.

....

....

....

4 a

WHAT WOULD YOU SAY?

You want some advice on sleeping better.

You say: ....

Someone asks for your advice on quitting smoking.

You say: ....

Someone asks you whether you prefer people who stay up late or people who go to bed early.

You say: ....

"Well, I'd probably need to ask for advice."

b Group Work Brainstorm ways to practice this language out of class. Imagine you are visiting an English-speaking country. Where/When might you need this language?

5 Out of Class Interview three people about someone they have lived with. Find out three good things and three not-so-good things and make notes. Bring the information to your next class and discuss it.

6 Vocabulary check. Check [√] the words you know.

Adjectives/Adverbs			Nouns			Verbs		Modals
☐ calming	☐ inappropriate	☐ often	☐ acupuncture	☐ hypnosis	☐ quantity	☐ compare	☐ quit	☐ might
☐ creative	☐ individual	☐ regularly	☐ advice	☐ insomniac	☐ ritual	☐ cure	☐ rest	☐ should
☐ essential	☐ irregular	☐ self-help	☐ caffeine	☐ motivation	☐ sleeplessness	☐ determine	☐ sacrifice	☐ shouldn't
☐ grumbling	☐ never	☐ trouble	☐ charity	☐ nap	☐ therapist	☐ dislike	☐ worry	
☐ hardly ever	☐ normal	☐ unusual	☐ comfort	☐ options	☐ workaholic	☐ encourage		
			☐ community center	☐ preferences		☐ kick		
				☐ quality		☐ prefer		

5 Review

Picture 1

Picture 2

Picture 3

Picture 4

A My brother insists on smoking in the apartment, even though he knows I hate it.

B Well, next time he does it, I would put on my warmest clothes and open all the windows and doors—that should cure him!

Task 1

a Use your imagination. Look at the pictures and decide which person is doing the following things. Write the number of the picture in the blank.

.... requesting information .... giving advice
.... expressing disbelief .... making an excuse

b Pair Work Compare responses with another student, giving reasons for your choices.

Task 2

a Look at these functions. Match them with the pieces of conversation listed below. Write the correct number in the blank.

.... requesting information
...../.... expressing disbelief
.... issuing an invitation
.... giving advice
.... responding to an invitation
.... expressing a preference

1 You're kidding me!
2 Well, next time he does it, I would . . .
3 I'm just calling up to see if you can . . .
4 Could you tell me where the . . .
5 You might like . . . but I like people who . . .
6 I would love to!

b Pair Work Think of a situation for each of these pieces of conversation. Make up two-line dialogues and practice them with a partner.

Task 3

a Listen. You will hear some people talking about problems and possible solutions. What are the solutions?

CONVERSATION	SOLUTIONS	PROBLEMS
1		
2		
3		
4		

b 🎧 Group Work Discussion. Listen again and decide what the problem is in each conversation. Write the problems in the chart.

c Pair Work Role play. Choose one of the problems and ask your partner for advice.

Task 4

a Pair Work You are at a party and you overhear someone say "I was there for two weeks before they rescued me."

On the blank lines below, write down the questions you would like to ask this person.

Who	?	When	?
What	?	Where	?
Why	?	How	?

b Group Work Exchange questions with another pair. Think of answers to their questions and then role play the situation.

Task 5

a Imagine you are talking to someone at the restaurant on the phone. In what order would you make these requests? Number them.

> **WHAT WOULD YOU SAY?**
>
> .... **To make a reservation at a restaurant**
>
> You say: ....
>
> .... **To ask for a table for two**
>
> You say: ....
>
> .... **To find out the address of the restaurant**
>
> You say: ....
>
> .... **To pay by credit card**
>
> You say: ....
>
> .... **To find out what time they open**
>
> You say: ....
>
> .... **To ask for a non-smoking table by the window**
>
> You say: ....

b Pair Work Write what you would say on the blank lines above.

c Pair Work Role play. Call up and have the conversation. Then change roles and practice again.

"Could you give me the telephone number of *Le Vent,* please?"

6 That's a Smart Idea

Unit Goals

In this unit you will:

Describe procedures

"The pictures should be arranged in a certain way."

Report what people say

"Tony asked if he could come over tomorrow."

A Well, that looks like a dog to me.

B A dog? I can't see anything in the picture at all.

Warm-Up

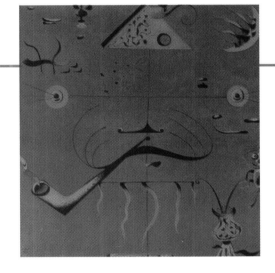

1 This painting is by the famous Catalunyan painter Joan Miró. How many different objects can you see in the picture?

2 **Group Work** Discussion. What problems are these inventions designed to solve?

a Floors that are wired so that when somebody drops their clothes, their books, or their toys, a buzzer goes off. If that person doesn't pick up their things in ten seconds, they get an electric shock.

b Telephones that tell teenagers that their 15 minutes are up and to go do their homework, and then disconnects them.

c Televisions that when the channel is changed more than 10 times in 10 minutes, will announce in a deep voice that the person watching should do something useful, like fix the sink. The set will then shut itself off and expel a puff of smoke.

d Alarm clocks that don't ring or play nice music. They squeal and shout threats and automatically back up out of your reach when you try to shut them off.

Task Chain 1 Creative work

LEARNING STRATEGY

Classifying = putting similar things together in groups.

Task 1

a PairWork Classify these words.

creative	logical	emotional	impulsive
analytical	holistic	calculating	intuitive

"Feeling" Words   *"Thinking" Words*

....
....
....
....

b GroupWork Discussion. Which qualities from Task 1a are important for the following occupations? (You can select as many qualities as you want.) Give reasons for your choices.

Occupation   *Qualities*
brain surgeon   ....
composer   ....
politician   ....
editor   ....
other: ....

Task 2

a 🎧 PairWork You will hear two creative people being interviewed about their work. Listen to the first part of the discussion and try to guess what they do. Use the chart to help you. Make a note of the key words that helped you decide.

	PROBABLE		POSSIBLE		IMPROBABLE	
	ROGER	INGRID	ROGER	INGRID	ROGER	INGRID
painter						
poet						
novelist						
musician						
songwriter						
sculptor						

b GroupWork Compare your responses with another pair and give reasons for your choices.

c 🎧 Now listen to the second part and decide what each person does.

Roger is a ....
Ingrid is a ....

d 🎧 Listen to the entire interview again. Which of the words from Task 1 can be associated with each person?

Roger ....
Ingrid ....

Task 3

a The following are parts of three employment advertisements. Match the ads and the companies below.

.... 1 theater company holding auditions for a national tour
.... 2 discotheque looking for a door person to keep out undesirables
.... 3 a private limousine company looking for drivers for unusual, late-night city tours

b What other qualities would these people need? Complete the ads.

c Pair Work Write your own advertisement for one of the following occupations. Exchange it with another pair and guess which occupation the advertisement is for.

computer programmer	dentist	painter
ballet dancer	language teacher	novelist
aerobics instructor	office assistant	architect
taxi driver		

Task 4

a What are the most creative things that you have done in the last:
month? ....
year? ....

b Group Work Talk about the things you did.

"Two weeks ago, I made a photo collage for a friend's birthday. Last year, I did a radio program at school with some of my friends."

Language Focus 1 — Passives: past and perfect forms

1 a In Task 2, Roger and Ingrid were asked about the creative process. Who do you think gave these answers? Write "R" for Roger or "I" for Ingrid.

1 .... The key words were written on cards, and the ones that rhymed were put together.
2 .... In most cases the lyrics were written after the tunes.
3 .... I've been asked to get it finished in time for the annual folk festival.
4 .... The lines were written dozens of times.
5 .... It's been recorded by three different groups now.

What's the first thing that happened in writing the poem?

b **Pair Work** Think of the questions that elicited these answers and practice them. The first one has been done for you.

2 **Pair Work** Trivia quiz. Choose what you think is the correct answer and then practice asking and answering questions.

Australia 1975	Canada 1940	the United States 1993
Brazil 1968	Thailand 1984	the United Kingdom 1989
Japan 1952	Hollywood	

A "Where was *West Side Story* first performed?"

B "I think it was first performed in New York."

QUESTION	ANSWER
1 When was the Rock Opera *Tommy* composed?	
2 Where was the compact disc invented?	
3 When was the second Woodstock Pop Festival staged?	
4 Where have most of the popular movies been made?	
5 When .... ?	
6 Where .... ?	

3 a The passive rather than active voice is used (1) when the action is more important than the person performing the action, and (2) when we don't know who performed the action. Why do you think that the passive was used in the following sentences? Write **1** or **2**.

.... I've been asked to appear on TV to talk about our new show.
.... We had to cancel the show because some of the instruments were stolen.
.... The show was given a great review in yesterday's newspaper.
.... A huge bunch of roses was left at the stage door.
.... The final song was finished a few hours before opening night.

b **Pair Work** Compare your responses with another student.

Task 1

a **Pair Work** You are about to read a magazine article entitled *Extraordinary Uses for Ordinary Things*. What do you think it will be about? Check [√] one.

☐ Recent inventions for solving everyday household problems
☐ Useful things to do with everyday objects
☐ The year's most extraordinary inventions

b Now read the article on page 48, and write the names of the following items in the appropriate spaces.

Plastic milk container

A can and a jar

A toothbrush

A newspaper

A container of salt

Extraordinary Uses for Ordinary Things

These are too useful to throw away even though they're too worn for their original purpose. Instead use them to:

- clean tiny corners and crevices, such as between bathroom tiles. They're also handy in the car to clean radio knobs and button controls.
- color small sections of your hair accurately.
- scrub away small stains from clothing.

Take the containers to your local recycling center. But what about the lids?

- They make neat saucers for houseplants.
- Small lids can be used as carpet protecters. Place under your furniture legs to prevent marking your carpet.
- The containers themselves can be cleaned and used to store flour, sugar, cookies, pasta, and rice.

- When painting, wet them and apply them to the window panes to keep them clean as you paint the woodwork. Afterwards just peel them off.
- Scrunched up, they are great for cleaning car windows. Wet the windshield, then scrub it down.

- Clean greasy pans by sprinkling a little on and then wiping away with paper.
- A little inside sneakers will absorb odors.

- Great for storing breakfast cereals.
- Ideal as a watering can.
- Make a funnel for pouring oil into the car. Cut the bottom off and turn it upside down.
- Can be used to store soup in the freezer.

Task 2

Group Work Brainstorm. How many additional uses can you think of for the items in the article?

Task 3

"I think that the solution is to buy the black socks."

a Listen to the conversation and identify the problem.

b Group Work Brainstorm. How many solutions can you think of for the problem?

c Now listen for Aunt Josephine's solution.

d Listen again. Her family objected to the innovative idea. Write their objections in the chart.

NAME	OBJECTION
1 Danielle	
2 Todd	
3 Lou	

e Think of a common, everyday problem (like losing one sock). Brainstorm ways of solving the problem, and then identify the pros and cons of each solution.

Language Focus 2 Reported speech

STORY 1

Cousin Danielle said that if the Velcro touched her skirt when she was sitting in class, and the teacher asked her to stand up, it would pull her skirt down. And Uncle Todd said that if he crossed his legs at the ankles, the socks would stick, and when he stood up, he'd fall flat on his face. Cousin Lou said that it wouldn't help him because he didn't have any matching socks anyway!

1 In Task Chain 2 you heard Josephine's niece tell the story at left. Now figure out the exact words that each person in the story used.

Example

Danielle: "If the velcro touches my skirt when I'm in class and the teacher asks me to stand up, it will pull my skirt down."

Todd: ....   Lou: ....

2 Change the following statements into reported speech. Then practice reporting what the people said.

Example

Aunt Josephine: "I can't stand the way this washing machine eats socks."

My aunt said that she couldn't stand the way that washing machine ate socks.

a Aunt Josephine: "I hate the way no one listens to my complaints."
She also said that ....

b Cousin Danielle: "Some people think Mom is eccentric."
My cousin said that ....

c Niece: "I think she's interesting."
I said that ....

d Niece: "She's always had novel solutions to problems."
I also said that ....

3 Look at the following story. Underline the words and phrases that talk about when something happened.

Do you know the rule?

Fill in the chart and compare it with another student. The first one has been done for you.

In reported speech:

this/these	becomes	that/those
here	becomes	....
today/tonight	becomes	....
yesterday	becomes	....
tomorrow	becomes	....
two days ago	becomes	....

STORY 2

Our English teacher was really mad at everyone the other day. He said that most students had done badly on the exam the day before. He said he'd warned us two days earlier about the exam. Then he said he was going to give us another exam the next day. One of the students asked him not to because there was a concert that night, and most of the students were going. That made the teacher even angrier. He warned us that he was going to give the exam anyway, and told everyone to be there on time.

Self-Check

COMMUNICATION CHALLENGE

PairWork Student A: Look at Challenge 6A on page 113. Student B: Look at Challenge 6B on page 116.

1 Write three new sentences or questions you learned.

....

....

....

2 The following are some of the strategies you practiced in this unit. How well can you do these things? Check [√] your answers and then compare with another student.

HOW WELL DID YOU DO?

	Excellent	Good	So-so	Need more practice
• **Selective listening** (listening for the most important words and information)	☐	☐	☐	☐
• **Classifying** (putting similar things together in groups)	☐	☐	☐	☐
• **Making inferences** (using information that is provided to learn new things that are not explicitly stated)	☐	☐	☐	☐

3 Out of Class *You choose:* Do Ⓐ or Ⓑ.

Ⓐ Interview friends and family and make a list of at least three practical problems they have around the home. Bring the list to class and brainstorm possible solutions to the problems.

Ⓑ Interview three friends or family members about what their "dream" occupation would be. Ask them what personal qualities they think are important for these occupations. Which of these qualities do they think that they possess?

4 Vocabulary check. Check [√] the words you know.

Adjectives/Adverbs
☐ accurately
☐ analytical
☐ calculating
☐ emotional
☐ employment
☐ everyday
☐ holistic

☐ ideal
☐ improbable
☐ impulsive
☐ innovative
☐ intuitive
☐ logical
☐ possible

☐ probable
☐ recycling
☐ smart

Nouns
☐ aerobics instructor
☐ architect
☐ ballet dancer
☐ bouncer
☐ buzzer
☐ computer programmer

☐ dentist
☐ disco
☐ event
☐ musician
☐ novelist
☐ painter
☐ poet
☐ procedure

☐ sculptor
☐ shock
☐ songwriter
☐ taxi driver
☐ Velcro

Verbs
☐ absorb
☐ back up
☐ disconnect

☐ pour
☐ scrub
☐ sprinkle

☐ store
☐ warn
☐ wire

7 Creatures Great and Small

Unit Goals

In this unit you will:

Give definitions

"Mammals are animals that have internal skeletons with backbones."

Express superlatives

"That is the most wonderful sight I have ever seen!"

Warm-Up

.... parrot .... cheetah .... dog

.... dolphin .... rabbit .... cat .... chimpanzee

1 a **Group Work** Which of these animals make good pets? Which make poor pets? Why? Rank them from best to worst (1 to 7).

b Do you have any pets? What kinds? What do you like or dislike about them?

2 a 🎧 **Group Work** Trivia quiz. Form teams, then listen to the questions and decide on the answers. Write the letter **A**, **B**, **C**; or **T** for true and **F** for false.

QUESTION	ANSWER
1	
2	
3	
4	
5	
6	

b Now check your answers on page 114.

3 **Group Work** Discussion.

a What is the most unusual creature you have ever seen?
b What do you think is the most aggressive animal on earth?
c What is the most beautiful insect you have seen?
d Where do the most mysterious creatures live?

"I think that the most mysterious creatures live at the bottom of the ocean."

Task Chain 1 If I could talk with the animals

Task 1

a How well do these animals communicate with each other? Check [√] column A. How well do they communicate with humans? Check [√] column B.

	A COMMUNICATE WITH EACH OTHER			B COMMUNICATE WITH HUMANS		
	Well	OK	Not well	Well	OK	Not well
dog						
dolphin						
chimpanzee						
parrot						
cat						
rabbit						
cheetah						

b Compare your responses with another student.

Task 2

a Listen to the conversation and identify the animal the people are talking about.

b Listen again. What is the topic of the conversation?

c Pair Work Compare responses, then listen once more to confirm your choices.

Task 3

a Skim this review of a television program and decide if the reviewer liked the program.

b Pair Work Compare responses with a classmate and give reasons for your choices.

c Group Work Discussion. Do you believe that animals have language? How convincing do you find the evidence discussed in the article?

Animal Talk

Interest in the issue of animal communication is on the increase, if the current offerings on television are anything to go by. In the last week, there have been no fewer than five programs dealing with the subject. The most interesting of these was a program aired late last night on TVPM. The programing executives obviously had little idea of the quality of the program, nor of the interest it would generate. It should have been aired in prime time.

The program provided a general look at the issue of animal communication, the basic question being: Do animals have language in the same way as humans have language? However, the show was quickly stolen by an African gray parrot named Nigel. We have all heard parrots talk, but do they have *language?* If we believe what this program showed, the answer must surely be a resounding "yes". Nigel is able to name wooden objects and toys that are pointed out by Irene Pepperberg, the woman who trained him. He can name different types of fruit in the same way.

Most remarkable of all, Nigel is able to communicate his feelings. On one occasion, after he gave a wrong answer, he lowered his head and apologized. Of course, the skeptics would say he has only learned these words as a collection of sounds, but those of us out here in TV land were delighted.

What made the show so delightful was the fact that the producers let Nigel tell his own story. There was no serious professor-type in the background telling us what to think on the issue of animal communication. This is what television is all about— letting words and pictures tell their own story without the interference of "experts." We don't need them to tell us what is obvious to our own eyes. ■

Task 4

a The following notes were made by two speakers preparing for a debate. The topic: Animals can communicate with humans in a meaningful way. Write **F** for *for* or **A** for *against* in the blank before each point to show whether or not it supports the statement.

.... Follow complex commands.
.... Fetch the newspaper on command.
.... Are not conscious of what they're saying.
.... Have no thought behind their actions—process of habit formation.
.... Require long period of training—complex actions broken down into sequence of simple ones.
.... Speak with their owners.

b Now match the opposing statements.

FOR	AGAINST
1	1
2	2
3	3

c **Group Work** Debate. Choose three speakers to speak in favor of, and three speakers to speak against the idea that animals can communicate meaningfully with humans. Each speaker speaks for two minutes, and the class then votes on which side presented the most convincing case.

Language Focus 1 Relative clauses with *that* and *whose*

A Reptiles are animals that . . .

B . . .have cold blood.

1 a Pair Work Student A: Say the first part of the statement. Student B: Complete the statement.

Student A
1 Reptiles are animals that . . .
2 Insects are animals that . . .
3 Mammals are animals that . . .
4 Birds are animals that . . .
5 Fish are animals that . . .

Student B
feed their young milk.
have warm blood.
are covered with feathers.
live in water.
eat flesh.
have cold blood.
have six legs.
can fly.
lay eggs.

b Pair Work Now change roles and do the task again.

2 a Combine these sentences following. The first one has been done for you.

Example: Mammals are animals. Mammals have warm blood.
"Mammals are animals that have warm blood."

1 Dinosaurs were reptiles. Dinosaurs ruled the earth for 160 million years.
2 Snakes are cold-blooded animals. Snakes live on land and in water.
3 Vertebrates are animals. They have a skeleton and a backbone.
4 Whales are mammals. Whales live in water.
5 Bats are vertebrates. They can fly.

b Pair Work Practice making statements using *that*.

3 Combine these sentences following the example.

Example: Mammals are animals. Their offspring have warm blood.
"Mammals are animals whose offspring have warm blood."

a Seals are water-dwelling mammals. Their offspring are born on land.
b Mammals are animals. Their young are fed on milk.
c Emus are birds. Their wings are too short to enable them to fly.
d Snakes are reptiles. Their skin is shed each year.

A This animal is a reptile that is now extinct.

B A dinosaur!

4 a Group Work Make up your own trivia quiz. Think of five descriptions like the one at left.

b Group Work Now compete with another group. Take turns asking and answering each other's trivia questions.

Task 1

a Check [√] the words you know.

☐ interesting   ☐ precious   ☐ beautiful
☐ magical   ☐ wonderful   ☐ exciting
☐ dramatic   ☐ incredible   ☐ difficult
☐ endangered

b **Pair Work** Compare responses with a partner.

c Which words could be used to describe the creatures in these pictures?

A hunting spider

A land crab

A human being

A tree kangaroo

Task 2

a 🎧 Listen to the inteview and circle the words in Task 1a that you hear.

b What does the naturalist say about these creatures?

hunting spider: ....
land crabs: ....
tree kangaroo: ....
human beings: ....

Task 3

These letters to the editor appeared in an Australian newspaper. Read the letters and note the points in favor of and the points against the protection of the tree kangaroo.

Dear Editor,

I read with disgust your article on the tree kangaroo. According to your article, the tree kangaroo is faced with extinction because of the destruction of its native habitat by "evil" logging companies. Well, I am the chief executive officer of the largest logging company in the Tatawangalo State Forest region, and I strongly disagree with some of the points that your reporter made.

Your article asserts that the tree kangaroo is an endangered species. This is untrue. I have seen three of these creatures in the last three weeks. My workers also report frequent sightings of the kangaroo.

Even if the tree kangaroo is in danger of extinction, this is not a good reason to stop cutting down trees. Species have been dying out ever since the planet first began to evolve. It's a natural process. When was the last time that you saw a dinosaur? The planet has been getting along quite nicely without these creatures for millions of years.

If logging were to be stopped, it would mean the extinction of loggers, who, in my view, are far more important than kangaroos. In my opinion, there is something seriously wrong with individuals who put animals before humans. And it's not just the loggers and their families who would suffer. We would all suffer. The economy, which is in pretty poor shape at the moment, depends heavily on the export of natural products such as our forest timbers.

In the future, you should think carefully before printing such a one-sided article.

Yours,
Humans Have Rights, Too, You Know

Dear Editor,

I was dismayed by the article in your newspaper on the possibility of the extinction of the tree kangaroo. Two years ago, I took my family on a camping holiday in the Tatawangalo State Forest. It is one of the happiest holidays that we've ever had—in one of the most beautiful places on earth. The only thing that shattered our peace was the constant noise of the loggers destroying the natural beauty of the place with their chain saws. While we were in the forest, we saw several of the delightful but very shy tree kangaroos. This was definitely the high point of the trip for my children. It fills me with sorrow and shame to think that *their* children might never have the chance to see these lovely creatures in their native habitat. People just don't seem to realize that once something is extinct it is lost forever.

I would like to close by thanking you for your article, and for making the public aware of the endangered tree kangaroo.

Sincerely,
Nature Lover

Task 4

a Select the letter you disagree with, and write a response. Summarize the points made in the letter, then state your objections to these, and give reasons.

b Exchange letters with a student who has expressed a different point of view from you, then discuss your differences of opinion.

Dear Humans Have Rights Too,

In your letter to the editor, you state that . . .
....
....

I believe that you are wrong for the following reasons:
....
....

Sincerely,

Language Focus 2 Superlative adjectives with present perfect

Do you know the rule?

a **Pair Work** Look back over the unit and make a list of adjectives that can fill the pattern:
What's the most (*adjective*) (*noun*) you've ever (*verb*)?

b When do we use *most + adjective* and when do we use *adjective + -est?*

"What's the most interesting thing you've ever done?"

"The most adventurous trip Tomoko has ever taken was a shopping trip to Macy's!"

"The most annoying thing that happened to us was being delayed at the airport before we left for Seoul."

1 **Pair Work** Match these questions and answers and then practice them with a partner.

Questions
a What's the most interesting thing you've ever done, Tom?
b What's the most beautiful sight you've ever seen, Sally?
c When's the best time to visit Thailand?
d What's the greatest experience Sam and Nadia have ever had?
e What's the most adventurous trip they've ever taken?
f Who's the most unusual person you've ever met?
g Why did you say that going to Mexico was the best vacation you've ever taken?

Answers
.... Going to a rock concert in Central Park.
.... A boat trip up the Amazon.
.... The culture, the food, the people, the climate, and the sights were perfect.
.... The guy who wrote the rock opera *Tommy.*
.... Learning how to paint.
.... I guess December, because it's not too hot.
.... Seeing the sun set over Manhattan from the top of Rockefeller Center.

2 **a** **Pair Work** Discussion. Ask and answer questions with your partner about the . . .
- most interesting thing they've ever done
- hardest thing they've ever done
- most beautiful sight they've ever seen
- most incredible experience they've ever had
- oldest movie they've ever seen
- most adventurous trip they've ever taken
- most unusual person they've ever met

b **Group Work** Tell another pair about your partner's experiences.

3 **a** **Pair Work** Discuss the following things that happened to you on a journey or vacation.
- the most interesting/unusual thing
- the best thing
- the most frightening thing
- the most unpleasant/worst thing
- the most annoying thing

b **Group Work** Tell another pair about your experiences.

Self-Check

COMMUNICATION CHALLENGE

Pair Work Student A: Look at Challenge 7A on page 115. Student B: Look at Challenge 7B on page 117.

1 Write three new sentences or questions you learned.

....

....

....

2 a Pair Work Here are some of the strategies you practiced in this unit. How well can you do these things? Check [√] your answers and then compare with another student.

HOW WELL DID YOU DO?

	Excellent	Good	So-so	Need more practice
• **Role playing** (pretending to someone else and using the right language for the situation you are in)	☐	☐	☐	☐
• **Skimming** (reading quickly to get a general idea of a text)	☐	☐	☐	☐
• **Choosing** (selecting the task you want to do from two alternatives)	☐	☐	☐	☐

b Group Work Brainstorm. Which of these strategies would you use out of class? Where? For what purposes?

3 Out of Class Visit a travel agency and collect information and any brochures in English describing interesting and unusual tours. Bring them to class and talk about them.

4 Vocabulary check. Check [√] the words you know.

Adjectives/Adverbs

☐ adventurous	☐ extinct	☐ remarkable
☐ aggressive	☐ extreme	☐ seriously
☐ complex	☐ magical	☐ shy
☐ convincing	☐ meaningfully	☐ surely
☐ delightful	☐ opposing	☐ unpleasant
☐ endangered	☐ precious	☐ wonderful

Nouns

☐ chimpanzee	☐ extinction	☐ mammal
☐ crab	☐ feelings	☐ offspring
☐ creature	☐ habitat	☐ parrot
☐ definition	☐ habit-formation	☐ reptile
☐ destruction		☐ sequence
☐ dinosaur	☐ insect	☐ skeptic
☐ disgust	☐ interest	☐ spider
☐ dolphin	☐ interference	☐ vertebrate
☐ eco-trip	☐ kangaroo	☐ whale

Verbs

☐ air	☐ name	☐ shed
☐ apologize	☐ rule	☐ skim
☐ communicate	☐ shatter	

8 Communications

Warm-Up

Unit Goals

In this unit you will:

Describe intentions

"I plan to give up trying to communicate with my neighbor—he's impossible."

Make indirect requests

"I wonder if you could help us design a new logo."

1 What methods of communication are these people using?

2 a Pair Work Think of several ways of completing the following statements.

"I find it really difficult communicating in the following situations:"

....

"I enjoy communicating in the following situations:"

....

b Group Work What makes communication easy? Difficult?

3 a Do you know English expressions for the following situations?

   1 showing that you don't understand
   2 checking that you have understood the other person
   3 checking that the other person has correctly understood you

b What are these people doing? Match each statement to a situation from Task 3a. Put the correct number in the blank.

   1 .... "Did you say she won a million bucks?"
   2 .... "Excuse me?"
   3 .... "Then you take a left off 21st Street. You know where I mean?"

"Last week I called my ex-girlfriend and left an invitation to lunch on her voice mail. But she never called back."

Task 1

a Survey. The following are all ways of communicating over a phone line. Check [√] the ones you use. For the devices you use write down how often you use them (twice a week, once a month, etc.). When was the last time you used each? Who did you communicate with? What did you communicate about? Fill in the chart.

	HOW OFTEN	WHEN	TO WHOM	ABOUT
☐ regular telephone				
☐ mobile telephone				
☐ answering machine				
☐ fax				
☐ voice mail				

b Group Work Compare your responses with three or four other students' responses.

Task 2

a Look at this page from the front of a telephone directory. Match the headings with the customer calling services described below.

Three-Way Calling   **Speed Calling**   **Call Waiting**
Call Forwarding   **Caller ID**

Customer Calling Services

These optional calling services are available in all of the exchanges in this directory to one-party service customers only.

■ ....
When you're on the phone, a beep tone lets you know if another person is calling you. The person calling you hears only the normal ringing. You can then put the first caller on hold and talk to the second caller.

■ ....
Lets you program your phone to dial frequently called local or long distance numbers by using just one or two digits.

■ ....
Lets you add a third person to your conversation whether or not you have received or placed the first call.

■ ....
Lets you transfer your incoming calls to another telephone number.

■ ....
Tells you the number of the person calling when your phone rings.

b Which telephone services would you recommend for the following people? (Some may need more than one service.)

1 Your sister runs a telephone dating service. People call her up, and she puts them in touch with other callers by phone.

2 Your brother runs a small direct-mail business from home. The warehouse that dispatches his products for him is often busy, and he wastes a lot of time trying to get through to them. He also has a lot of incoming and outgoing calls.

3 Your neighbor runs a window-cleaning service. He is out on the road most of the day.

4 Your elderly aunt is confined to her home. Her only means of communicating is through the telephone, which she finds difficult because she has arthritis (a disease of the joints) in her hands.

c PairWork Compare answers and give reasons for your choices.

d GroupWork Discussion. Which of these services would you like? Rank them from most to least useful (1–5). Give reasons.

Task 3

a 🎧 Listen to the three conversations and decide which of the Customer Calling Services is being used in each case.

CONVERSATION	CUSTOMER CALLING SERVICE
1	
2	
3	

b 🎧 PairWork Compare responses with another student and then listen again to check your answers.

Task 4

You choose: Do Ⓐ or Ⓑ.

Ⓐ **a** PairWork You and your partner are going into business together. Decide what kind of business you are starting, and then decide which of the telephone services from Task 2 you would like to have.

Ⓑ **a** Select one of the calling services from Task 2, and think of reasons why the service is valuable.

b PairWork You are a telephone company sales representative. Try to convince your partner to get the calling service you selected.

Language Focus 1 — Two-part verbs + gerunds

1 Rewrite the following sentences. Replace each underlined two- or three-part verb with one of these verbs: *postpone, tolerate, stop, continue.*

a I'm not going to <u>keep on</u> calling someone who never calls back.

b Steve says that he's going to <u>give up</u> trying to fax the West Coast office. He can never get through.

c I've <u>put off</u> calling Sally because I'll have to tell her she didn't get the promotion she was after.

d We're moving because we can't <u>put up with</u> those noisy neighbors.

2 a Fill in the blanks with the appropriate two-part verbs.

keep on **giving up** **looks forward to**

When faced with a difficult communication situation, different people react in different ways. Some people .... talking as though nothing unusual had happened. Others avoid conflict whenever it occurs. Occasionally you meet someone who .... participating in difficult situations, seeing these as a challenge. A few people deal with the situation by .... communicating completely.

b PairWork Check your responses with another student's responses.

3 a Think of an appropriate response to the following statements and questions using the verb in parentheses.

Example: "I thought you were going to stop smoking this year?"
(give up) "I am. I give up smoking every year."

1 I hear you've finally accepted that new job.
(look forward to) ....

2 Our phone bill was huge this month.
(cut down on) ....

3 Did the boss fire that incompetent worker yet?
(not go through with) ....

4 I see that you booked a court at the tennis club.
(take up) ....

b PairWork Now practice them with another student.

4 a Think of plans and intentions you have and complete these statements.

1 I plan to keep on ....

2 I think I'll cut down on ....

3 I'm not going to put off ....

4 I think I'll take up ....

5 I plan on ....

b PairWork Now practice the statements with a partner.

Task Chain 2 Image makers!

"Well, a logo says a lot about a company. So does the slogan that they use."

Task 1

a What is a "logo?" Find the derivation of the word in your dictionary.

b **Pair Work** Look at these logos. What "message" does each convey? Make a list of several words to describe each logo.

c **Group Work** Compare your list with another pair. Discuss what kinds of companies these logos might belong to.

Task 2

Group Work In the next task you will listen to a communications consultant talking about his work with large corporations. Discuss the ways in which corporations and other organizations communicate information about themselves.

Task 3

a 🎧 Listen to the tape and identify the two corporations being discussed, the problem each one had, and the solution.

CORPORATION	PROBLEM	SOLUTION
1		
2		

b 🎧 **Pair Work** Listen again and find the logos for the corporations that are mentioned.

Task 4

a **Group Work** Role play. Select one of the following scenarios and brainstorm solutions for the problem. Try to think of as many different solutions as you can, and then decide on the best one.

Scenario 1: You work for a company that is trying to break into a market in another country. The company has a strong public image—an image closely associated with the logo, company slogan, and advertising campaign. Unfortunately, your logo has negative connotations in the new country. If you keep the logo, slogan, and advertisements, it is unlikely that the product will be accepted in this new country. If you change them, your corporate image will suffer at home and elsewhere abroad.

Scenario 2: You work for a company that produces luxury motor vehicles. Several of the vehicles have been found to have faulty braking systems. All the vehicles should be recalled for inspection. However, the company is afraid to place advertisements in the media calling for the return of the cars because its image will suffer.

Scenario 3: You work for a company that manufactures clothing. Due to increased competition, sales have fallen, and the company has laid off some of its workers. This has led to a general drop in morale, which is further damaging the ability of your company to compete. If you could guarantee workers there will be no more lay-offs, morale would increase. However, while you hope that there will be no more lay-offs, you cannot guarantee this.

b **GroupWork** Compare your solutions with the solutions of a group that has worked on a different problem. Discuss the different types of solutions.

Task 5

"Well, the first one might be used to sell soap, health food, deodorant, skin cream, or even mineral water."

a **PairWork** Most of the identifying words have been removed from these advertisements. Make a list of the things that each ad might be used for to sell. Can you guess any of the words that have been removed?

A simple and straight-forward .... and fitness line created by .... for today's active, health-focused lifestyles. These are no-nonsense, nutrient-based products that protect and condition your .... Like a .... with .... Or an all-over .... and body .... that's sweat-resistant, water resistant, and fortified with .... Plus a .... to keep you .... and .... Pure. Basic. Easy.

It's not for everyone. But isn't that the beauty of it? It's one thing to be wanted by all. It's quite another to be obtainable by only a few. The .... is decidedly the latter. With a bias towards luxury, the .... is a study in elegance. It abounds with refinements, from the .... to the .... on the .... and .... Its .... give it the responsive agility you demand of a .... And it has the .... features .... you would expect from a .... of this caliber. Which can be a beautiful thing in itself. Some things are worth the price.

b **GroupWork** Compare your responses with another pair, then comment on each other's ideas.

c **GroupWork** Discussion. The companies in Task 5a have tried to create a distinctive corporate image through their advertisements. What kind of image are the ads trying to promote (quality, value, environmentally-friendly, etc.)? Which words and phrases are used to achieve this? What age group are the ads aimed at? What social group? Which image appeals to you?

Language Focus 2 Indirect questions & requests

1 Change these direct requests into indirect questions.

Example:
"I wonder if you could help us to design a new corporate logo?"
"Could you help us to design a new corporate logo?"

a Can you let us know how expensive it will be?

....

b Do you think it will make a difference to our image?

....

c When do you think you could have it done?

....

d What do you imagine the problem with our image is?

....

e Do you know if the new logo is ready?

....

2 **Pair Work** Now practice them with a partner.

3 **Pair Work** One student takes the A role and the other takes the B role.

Student A
a Add three items to the following hypothetical situations, and then use them to make requests.

1 Your apartment is being painted and you have to get out for a few days.
2 Your family is visiting and you have no room for them in your apartment.
3 You need to pay a large bill, but are temporarily out of money.
4 ....
5 ....
6 ....

b Now change roles and do the task again.

Student B
a Your partner is going to make a number of unusual requests. Reply to each request.
b Now use your own three additional items and change roles.

4 a Write several requests that you would like another student to make.

b **Pair Work** Exchange requests with another student and go around the class and make the requests.

"I wonder if I could move in with you for a few days?"

"I'm sorry, my parents are here for the weekend."

"Would you ask Yumiko if she could bring her book on Zen to school tomorrow?"

A Yumiko, can you bring your book on Zen to school for Alan tomorrow?

B Unfortunately, I don't have it any more—I left it on the bus last week.

Self-Check

COMMUNICATION CHALLENGE

Group Work Student A: Look at Challenge 8A on page 117. Student B: Look at Challenge 8B on page 118. Student C: Look at Challenge 8C on page 120.

1 Write three new sentences or questions you learned.

....

....

....

2 These are some of the strategies you practiced in this unit. How well can you do these things? Check [√] your answers and then compare with another student.

HOW WELL DID YOU DO?

	Excellent	Good	So-so	Need more practice
• **Selective listening** (listening for the most important words and information)	☐	☐	☐	☐
• **Practicing** (listening or reading and repeating—practicing improves your fluency and makes you a better speaker)	☐	☐	☐	☐
• **Memorizing conversational patterns** (learning phrases to start conversations and keep them going)	☐	☐	☐	☐

3 Out of Class Find examples of advertisements that are being used to develop particular images for the products they are selling. These can be in English or in your own language. Bring them to class and discuss the image the company is trying to project, how they have tried to do this, and how successful they have been.

4 Vocabulary check. Check [√] the words you know.

Adjectives/Adverbs
☐ confined
☐ corporate
☐ difficult
☐ distinctive
☐ environmentally- friendly
☐ faulty
☐ further
☐ identifying
☐ incompetent
☐ increased
☐ indirect
☐ luxury
☐ negative
☐ obtainable
☐ occasionally
☐ valuable

Nouns
☐ answering machine
☐ calling services
☐ communications
☐ connotation
☐ consultant
☐ corporation
☐ dating service
☐ elegance
☐ expression
☐ fax
☐ image
☐ intentions
☐ latter
☐ logo
☐ manufacturer
☐ mobile phone
☐ morale
☐ plan
☐ quality
☐ scenario
☐ slogan
☐ solutio
☐ products
☐ voice mail

Verbs
☐ compare
☐ confirm
☐ continue
☐ convey
☐ convince
☐ design
☐ dispatch
☐ forward
☐ postpone
☐ rank
☐ recommend
☐ stop
☐ tolerate
☐ transfer

Phrasal Verbs
☐ call up
☐ cut down on
☐ get through
☐ get out
☐ give up
☐ go through with
☐ keep on
☐ lay off
☐ look forward to
☐ move in
☐ plan on
☐ put off
☐ put up with
☐ stay in
☐ take up

9 Helping Hands

Pledge me!
WALK FOR HUNGER!

Unit Goals

In this unit you will:

Ask others to do things

"I'd like you to support Greenpeace."

"I want you to take a few minutes to read this brochure."

Make excuses

"I'm sorry, but I seem to be out of cash right now."

Talk about hypothetical situations in the past

"If it had been me, I'd have changed jobs."

"Well, I think that the first picture has to do with raising money for education."

Warm-Up

Picture 1

Picture 2

Picture 3

Picture 4

1 Group Work These pictures are from organizations that raise money for different causes. Can you think of a cause for each of these pictures?

2 a Group Work Discussion. These are excerpts from letters asking for money for charitable causes. Can you match each excerpt with a picture?

.... Just ten dollars will feed a child for . . .
.... is now a major health issue in every country in the . . .
.... We need your help to save the endangered . . .
.... to provide books and materials for those who can't afford them.

b Pair Work Take turns making the excerpts into complete sentences.

Task Chain 1 — A charitable cause

LEARNING STRATEGY

Brainstorming = thinking of as many new words and ideas as you can.

A Let's have a 24-hour fast to raise money for Oxfam.

B How does that work?

A Well, you get friends and family to sponsor you. They donate a dollar for every hour you can last without food.

Task 1

a Read the following text and match it with a picture from page 67.

> On May 8, you may be taking your mother out to lunch to thank her for her years of devotion to your health and happiness. This year, for the cost of that meal, you could give a Mother's Day gift to hundreds of mothers in the developing world. Women who care as much about their children as your mother does about you, but who have to fight hard every day just to find enough food to feed them. But you can help change that with a donation to Oxfam in your mother's name. Oxfam teaches women to read and write, helps them to improve their livestock-raising skills, and offers loans to launch a family business. All this benefits the whole community. This Mother's Day, don't just take your mother out to lunch. Give her a gift she'll really appreciate—the opportunity to help change the lives of mothers around the world. For every donation received by May 3, we will send you a special card to give your mother for Mother's Day on May 8.

b Group Work Brainstorm. Think of other ways of supporting causes such as Oxfam.

Task 2

a 🎧 Listen. You will hear four people raising money for charitable causes. Match the conversations and the pictures.

Conversation ....

Conversation ....

Conversation ....

Conversation ....

b 🎧 Listen again. What is the name of each charity? What kind of work does the charity do?

PERSON	NAME OF CHARITY	WORK IT DOES
Linda		
Mike		
Martha		
Peter		

c 🎧 **Pair Work** Listen once more and note the reactions of the people being approached. Complete these statements.

People's Reactions

.... **1** The person approached by Linda reacted by ....

.... **2** The person approached by Mike reacted by ....

.... **3** The person approached by Martha reacted by ....

.... **4** The person approached by Peter reacted by ....

"Well, I think that . . . got the most favorable reaction."

"I agree. And . . . got the least favorable reaction."

d **Pair Work** Rank the reactions from most to least favorable (1 to 4).

e **Group Work** Discussion. Whose views are most like or least like yours? How would you have reacted in each case?

Task 3

a Which of the following causes do you think is the most important internationally? Which is most important in your country?

b **Group Work** Can you add to the list? Now fill in the chart by putting a check [√] to rate the importance of each cause.

	IN YOUR COUNTRY			INTERNATIONALLY		
	a little	no	yes	a little	no	yes
World hunger						
Saving the environment						
Research into public health problems						
Helping political prisoners						
....						
....						

c **Group Work** Discuss your choices. Give reasons.

Task 4

a **Group Work** Brainstorm. Make a list of all the things in your school or neighborhood that you could collect money for.

b **Group Work** Now brainstorm ideas for raising money for one of these causes (a fun run, a walkathon, an art exhibition).

c **Group Work** Compare ideas. Which group had the most interesting ones?

Task 5

a Write a letter seeking support for one of the causes from Task 3.

b **Pair Work** Exchange letters and write a response.

Dear Community Member,

Tania Koslowski is one of the most gifted athletes our school has ever seen. She has just been selected for the International Junior Athletics meet in Helsinki. We want you to consider sponsoring Tania to go to Helsinki in July.

We ....

....

....

....

Language Focus 1 Object + infinitive

1 a Match these requests and responses.

Requests

1 I'd like you just to read this promotional brochure.
2 I want you to think about giving to the Freedom from Hunger Campaign.
3 We need everyone to sign the petition on human rights.
4 I want you to talk to your friends about the Environmental Aid Appeal.
5 I'd like you and Alicia to help us raise money for the library fund.
6 They want us to take part in the charity concert.

Responses

.... I'm afraid they think it's a waste of money.
.... Oh, dear, I don't have my glasses with me.
.... I thought they only wanted people with talent.
.... I'm not sure that we have the time.
.... But Gina and Andre aren't here today.
.... I already did—last week.

b Pair Work Now practice the requests and responses with a partner.

"We wanted the teachers to support our school bus campaign."

2 a Look at the chart in Task 2b (page 68) and complete these statements following the model at left.

1 Linda wanted ....
2 The person talking to Mike wanted ....
3 Martha asked ....
4 Peter said ....

b Pair Work Compare your answers. (You may listen again if necessary.)

A I'd like you to call the bank for me.

B I'm sorry, the phone is out of order.

3 Pair Work Think of requests that might elicit these excuses.

a I'm sorry, the phone is out of order.
b Oh, there's my bus. I've got to run.
c I left my planner at home, but I think I'm busy next Tuesday night.
d I'm not going to school tomorrow either.
e I'd love to, but my wife wouldn't approve.

4 a Make notes on what you would have to say to do these things.

1 Ask a stranger to donate to a charity that helps homeless children.
2 Get a friend to help you collect money for your favorite charity.
3 Get the rest of the class to take part in a walk against cancer.

b Group Work Now take turns role playing each situation.

Task Chain 2 Harry the helper

Task 1

a Group Work Imagine that you are one of these people. Make up a story about the picture and tell it to the group.

b Select the most interesting/funniest story and tell it to the class. Which group has the best story?

Task 2

a 🎧 Listen to the conversation. Which of the incidents in Task 1 are described?

b 🎧 Listen again and fill in the chart.

"If Harry hadn't helped the VIP, he'd have been . . . "

INCIDENT	WHAT HAPPENED	WHAT HARRY DID
VIP		
groom		
celebrity		

c Pair Work Take turns saying what would have happened if Harry hadn't helped.

Task 3

a GroupWork Working with two other students, complete the second paragraph of the following newspaper account using one of the incidents from Task 2. (Each student chooses a different incident.)

Special Award to Harry the Helper

SANTA MONICA The United Hoteliers Association held its 40th Annual Awards Dinner at the Santa Monica Prince Hotel yesterday. A highlight of the evening was the presentation of a special award to Harry Marciano, known throughout the industry as "Harry the Helper." After more than 50 years in the hotel business, Harry has finally decided to hang up his tie and tails. The award was given to Harry in recognition of his years of service, and for bringing new standards of service to the industry.

In making the award, Association President Ruth DeVries recounted several of Harry's better-known exploits. For instance, there was the time that

....
....
....
....
....
....
....
....
....
....

b GroupWork Use your paragraphs to produce a complete article.

c GroupWork Compare articles with another group.

Task 4

a GroupWork Think of someone you know who deserves an award for helping others. Tell the group about this person, giving reasons why he or she should be honored.

b GroupWork Vote on the most deserving person and think of an appropriate award for them.

Task 5

GroupWork Think of a time that you have been helped by someone else. Tell the story to the group. Describe (1) the problem you had, (2) the help you received, and (3) what would/wouldn't have happened if you hadn't gotten help.

"I once went to visit a friend in a strange town and he'd gone away for the weekend. I didn't have enough money to stay in a hotel, and I would have been in big trouble if a nice couple hadn't let me stay in their apartment overnight."

Language Focus 2 Past conditional

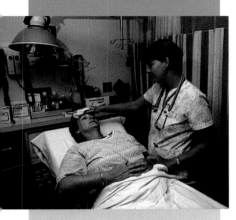

1 PairWork Match the two halves of the statements and practice them.

a If I hadn't become a nurse,
b If I'd become an attorney,
c If I'd stayed in social work,
d If I hadn't gone into teaching,
e If I'd stayed in school,

  .... I would have become rich.
  .... I wouldn't have ended up in this dead-end job.
  .... I wouldn't have gotten to work with young people.
  .... I would probably have become a social worker.
  .... I would have worked mostly with elderly people.

2 GroupWork Compare your responses with three other students.

3 PairWork Some of these sentences are incorrect. Correct them and practice them with a partner.

a I would have made a lot of money if I has stayed in advertising.
b If he had become an attorney, George was a wealthy man today.
c If we had left when I said, we wouldn't have the accident.
d I wouldn't have gone into medicine if I'd known how stressful it was.
e You wouldn't have the job if you hadn't been so convincing in the interview.

A Sergio won half a million dollars and spent it all in a year.

B If it had been me, I'd have spent it all in six months.

4 PairWork Respond to each of the following statements following the model at left.

a Peter got fired, and did nothing about it.
b George was in an accident that was caused by the other person, but decided not to sue.
c Tina left her job because she had too far to commute.
d The airline lost Alison's suitcase on her trip to Mexico, and she never got it back.
e When I accepted the job, they only gave me half the salary they had promised.

"I guess the most important decision I ever made was emigrating. If I hadn't moved to Canada, I would never have learned English."

5 a PairWork What are the three most important decisions you have ever made? What would have happened/not happened if you hadn't made that decision? Tell your partner.

b GroupWork Tell another pair about your partner's situation.

Self-Check

COMMUNICATION CHALLENGE

Look at Challenge 9 on page 118.

1 Write three new sentences or questions you learned.

....

....

....

2 The following are some of the strategies you practiced in this unit. How well can you do these things? Check [√] your answers and then compare with another student.

HOW WELL DID YOU DO?

	Excellent	Good	So-so	Need more practice
• **Personalizing** (sharing your own opinions, feelings, and ideas about a subject)	☐	☐	☐	☐
• **Brainstorming** (thinking of as many new words and ideas as you can)	☐	☐	☐	☐
• **Cooperating** (sharing ideas with other students and learning together)	☐	☐	☐	☐

3 Out of Class *You choose:* Do **A** or **B**.

A Collect some material from various charitable organizations or groups. Bring these to class and tell the class about them. Say how they raise money and what they do with the money.

B Find somebody who has been helped out of a difficult situation. Make notes and recount the story to the class.

4 Vocabulary check. Check [√] the words you know.

Adjectives/Adverbs

☐ charitable	☐ health	☐ sleepwalking
☐ developing	☐ helper	☐ terrible
☐ endangered	☐ homeless	☐ underprivileged
☐ favorable	☐ hypothetical	
☐ gifted	☐ promotional	

Nouns

☐ appeal	☐ charity	☐ human rights
☐ attorney	☐ devotion	
☐ award	☐ excerpt	☐ petition
☐ brochure	☐ famine	☐ recognition
☐ cause	☐ happiness	☐ relief

Verbs

☐ appreciate	☐ change	☐ promise
☐ approach	☐ commute	☐ raise
☐ approve	☐ donate	☐ react
☐ benefit	☐ help	☐ sponsor
☐ brainstorm	☐ lose	☐ support

10 Review

Task 1

a Underline the words that appeared in Unit 7. Look the others up in your dictionary.

	People	Places	Animals
unusual	☐	☐	☐
exotic	☐	☐	☐
bizarre	☐	☐	☐
extraordinary	☐	☐	☐
ridiculous	☐	☐	☐
frightening	☐	☐	☐
popular	☐	☐	☐
evil	☐	☐	☐
endangered	☐	☐	☐
....	☐	☐	☐
....	☐	☐	☐
....	☐	☐	☐

b Which of these words could you use to describe people, places, or animals? Put a check [√] in the appropriate box.

c Pair Work Add three words of your own to the list, and then practice making statements about the pictures.

"The man in the cloak is the most frightening person I've ever seen."

Task 2

a Look at these functions. Match them with the pieces of conversation listed below. Write the correct number in the blank.

.... expressing a superlative
.... reporting what someone else said
.... giving a definition
.... making an indirect request
.... making an excuse
.... talking about a hypothetical situation

1 . . . if you could help us to . . .
2 . . . delinquents are kids whose parents . . .
3 . . . I'm sorry but . . .
4 . . . that she had called the day before . . .
5 . . . I wouldn't have been able to buy . . .
6 . . . the most wonderful gift that . . .

b Pair Work Think of a situation for each of the phrases. Make up two-line conversations and practice them.

Task 3

a  Listen. You will hear people talking about three inventions. In the chart, make a note of the inventions and the reasons why they were invented.

INVENTION	WHY INVENTED
1	
2	
3	

b **Pair Work** Now make statements about each invention using the model at left.

"The . . . was invented/created/devised . . ."

Task 4

a Study the following responses to some indirect requests. Think of appropriate requests and write them in the spaces provided.

A I wonder if you'd like to play tennis on Saturday?

B I'm sorry, but it's my boyfriend's birthday.

Indirect Request	*Response*
1	"I'm afraid I can't. I just used the last one myself."
2	"Sure. I'll pick them up after school."
3	"Not at all. Here you are."
4	"I'm sorry, but my parents are visiting this weekend."
5	"I'm sorry, but I need it myself today."

b **Pair Work** Practice the requests and responses.

Task 5

a **Pair Work** Read this letter and take turns saying what you would have done in each situation.

b **Group Work** Ask group members about unfortunate things that have happened to them and say what you would have done in those situations.

It was the worst vacation ever. We arrived at the airport, and they wouldn't let us board the plane because neither of us had visas for Australia (our travel agent had told us we didn't need them!) So ....

When we finally got there, we discovered that because of a strike, there was no transportation into the city ....

Our problems continued when we got to the hotel. Because our flight had been delayed, the hotel had given away our room, and they said that they were completely booked. So we decided to ....

After everything was figured out, we got to our room, and I discovered that I'd left my briefcase with my computer and all my papers in the taxi. ....

11 Speaking Personally

Unit Goals

In this unit you will:

Ask for personal information
"What do you enjoy doing most?"

Express attitudes and opinions
"I think that growing up in a happy, secure environment is more important than growing up in a wealthy environment."

"In five years, the guy at the desk will be retired."

Warm-Up

1 Group Work Discussion. Look at these people. What are they doing? What do you think they'll be doing . . .

- in a few minutes?
- next week?
- next year?
- in five years?

2 Group Work Discussion. What do you think that you will be doing in the time periods listed above?

3 a Select three words from this list that best describe you.

ambitious	relaxed	aggressive	tense	easygoing
intense	patient	hard-working	fun-loving	competitive
friendly	lazy	impatient		

b Now compare your evaluations with another student.

c Which of these words do you think describe the people in the pictures?

Task Chain 1 Talking about ourselves

"Well, I'd ask what clothes they like to wear when they're relaxing, because that says a lot about someone's personality—you know, if they're laid back or not."

"What do I like doing more than anything else? Just hanging out with my friends, I guess."

Task 1

a **PairWork** Discussion. What qualities would you look for in someone you were going to . . .

- go on a vacation with?
- share an apartment with?
- complete a work/school project with?
- buy a car from?

b **PairWork** What questions would you ask to identify these qualities?

Task 2

a Answer the following questions.

1 What do you enjoy doing more than anything else?
2 What is your greatest ambition in life?
3 What is your greatest achievement so far?
4 Who do you admire most in the world, and why?
5 What is the best thing that has ever happened to you?
6 What is the most exciting thing that has ever happened to you?

b **PairWork** Compare your responses with another student's responses.

c Add two questions to the list in Task 2a and survey another student.

Task 3

a 🎧 Listen to the tape and make a note of the answers these people give to the questions.

QUESTION	MARK	VANESSA	SYLVIA
1			
2			
3			
4			
5			
6			

b Which person is most like you? Which person is least like you?

d where
ou're invited . . . go to the movies! do you like
meet me for lunch
what do you do?
why
s my family neighborhood

c GroupWork Discussion. Work with three or four other students and complete this survey.

		MARK			VANESSA			SYLVIA	
Which of these people would you . . .	YES	MAYBE	NO	YES	MAYBE	NO	YES	MAYBE	NO
go on a vacation with?									
share an apartment with?									
complete a work/school project with?									
buy a car from?									

LEARNING STRATEGY

Role playing = pretending to be someone else and using the right language for the situation you are in.

d GroupWork Think of questions you would like to ask each person. Role play the questions and answers.

Task 4

a PairWork The following resume was written by Mark, Vanessa, or Sylvia. Write his/her name in the blank space.

.... Byrne

2618 Calcaterra Drive
Santee, California 92071

EDUCATION   1989— High School Diploma, Mosswood High School

1991— Diploma in graphic design, San Jose Vocational College

EXPERIENCE   1992–1993 Trainee designer, Graphart Design, San Francisco

1993–1994 Designer and editor, Latin America Editores, Mexico City

1994 to present Graphic designer, In Press, San Jose

INTERESTS   Music of all kinds, modern literature, painting, languages, and travel.

b GroupWork Write your own resume but don't put your name on it. Give it to the teacher and take someone else's resume. Can you guess who wrote the resume you have?

Language Focus 1 *Wh-* questions + gerund/infinitive

1 Pair Work Take turns asking and answering these questions.

a What did you consider doing after graduation?
b Where do you intend to go for your next vacation?
c What did you want to be when you grew up?
d When do you enjoy playing sports?
e Where do you hope to live eventually?
f What kind of music do you dislike listening to most?
g When do you expect to stop taking English classes?
h Where would you suggest going this weekend?
i What chores would you avoid doing if you had the choice?

2 Use the correct form of 'do' (*doing* or *to do*) to complete these statements.

a What did you expect her .... about her job?
b When did he avoid .... the personality survey?
c What did you deny .... yesterday?
d Why did you suggest .... more studying this weekend?
e How did he expect you .... your homework?

3 a Some of these questions are incorrect. Correct them.

1 What do you suggest to do tonight?
2 What do you enjoy to do most on your vacation?
3 Who would you consider bringing to the party?
4 When do you hope going out?
5 What is something you dislike doing by yourself?
6 How could you deny to be at the party when everyone saw you?

b Pair Work Now practice them by asking and responding to the questions with another student.

4 a Pair Work Make up your own survey using these words plus a gerund (verb + *ing*) or infinitive (*to* + verb).

Who	do/did you	avoid	.... ?
What	do/did you	expect	.... ?
Where	do/did you	hope	.... ?
When	do/did you	consider	.... ?
Why	do/did you	intend	.... ?
How	do/did you	dislike	.... ?
		enjoy	.... ?
		want	.... ?

b Group Work Survey another pair.

c Group Work Now report the results to a third pair.

Do you know the rule?

Study the examples in this Language Focus and fill in the chart.

Always followed by gerund (-ing)

Example:
finish ....
....
....
....

Always followed by infinitive (to + verb)

Example:
appear ....
....
....
....
....

"Rama expects to go to the tennis tournament this weekend."

Task 1

a Pair Work A number of famous people were questioned about their childhood and the things that influenced them. Here are their responses. Can you think of the questions?

1 .... ? "A bike, when I was six years old."
2 .... ? "My mother, because she taught me to get the most out of every day."
3 .... ? "I guess being part of a large happy family."
4 .... ? "Being the only girl in a house full of boys."
5 .... ? "My grandparents' farm."
6 .... ? "Being in a bad car accident when I was around fourteen."

b Pair Work Take turns asking your partner some of the questions. Give answers that are true for you.

Task 2

a 🎧 Listen. You will hear three short conversations. What do/did these people want to do? What things influenced them? Fill in the chart.

NAME	WANTED TO DO/ INFLUENCES	AGE	CURRENT OCCUPATION
Ellie			
Charles			
Mary			

b 🎧 Listen again. Can you guess how old each speaker is? What do you think each person does (or, if it is a child, is likely to do)? Write your answers in the chart.

c Group Work Compare your results, and give reasons.

Task 3

a Skim the text on page 82 and decide which of the following it is. Check [√] one.
☐ a review of a TV program
☐ a magazine article
☐ an excerpt from a book

b Group Work Discussion. Discuss your choice with several other students. What helped you to decide?

Have you ever thought about what determines the way we are as adults? Remember the documentary series Seven Up? It started following the lives of a group of children in 1963. We first meet them as wide-eyed seven-year-olds and then catch up with them at seven-year intervals: giggling 14-year-olds, earnest 21-year-olds, then mature young adults.

Some of the stories are inspiring, others tragic, but what is striking in almost all the cases is the way in which the children's early hopes and dreams are reflected in their adult lives. For exmple, at seven, Tony is a lively child who says he wants to become a jockey or a taxi driver. When he grows up, he goes on to do both. How about Nicki, who says, "I'd like to find out all about the moon" and goes on to become a rocket scientist. As a child, soft-spoken Bruce says he wants to help "poor children" and ends up teaching in India.

But if the lives of all the children had been this predictable the program would be far less interesting than it actually was. It was the children whose childhood did not prepare them for what was to come that made the documentary so fascinating. Where did their ideas come from about what they wanted to do when they grew up? Are childen influenced by what their parents do, by what they see on television, or by what their teachers say? How great is the impact of a single inspirational event? Many film directors, including Stephen Spielberg, say that an early visit to the local cinema was the turning point in their lives.

Dr. Margaret McAllister, an educational psychologist, confirms that the major influences tend to be parents, friends, and the wider society. "When children first become aware of work, their early choices are unrealistic," says McAllister, "but as they get older, they start to make more realistic choices. Children turn to key role models for inspiration. If we look at imaginative play, it's very common that children play as moms and dads, then once they're at school, teaching becomes a popular choice—they've identified with the teacher, someone who is powerful, in control, and kind."

c **GroupWork** Discussion. What is the main point of the text? What evidence is provided to support that point? Do you agree or disagree? From your own experience, can you think of any evidence for or against the point?

Task 4

"My grandmother was one of the most influential people in my life because she taught me to get the most out of every single day. The place where we took family vacations was important because it was there that I finally learned to be independent. And graduating from college was important because it enabled me to have the career I wanted."

a What have been the three most influential people, places, and events in your life so far? Write in the space provided.

PEOPLE	PLACES	EVENTS
my grandmother	where we took family vacations	graduating from college

b **GroupWork** Now talk about why these people, places, and events were so important.

Language Focus 2 Comparative/superlative + gerund/infinitive

1 Pair Work Match these questions and answers and practice them.

Questions

a What did you enjoy most about your early life?
b Why do you say that your teen-age years were boring?
c What was the most important influence on you as a child?
d Why do you say that you fell into this career almost by accident?
e Why do you say you had a more fortunate upbringing than your friends?

Answers

.... Well, it was better to have grown up on a farm, like I did, than in a city apartment, like most of them.

.... There were fewer interesting things to do ten years ago than there are today.

.... Well, for most of my life I'd wanted to be an actor more desperately than a director.

.... The best thing was thinking about what it would be like being an adult.

.... I think being raised by the most artistic and creative parents in the world was the most significant thing.

2 a Complete the following statements using comparatives (*more*) and superlatives (*the most*).

1 Spending a week on a cruise ship in the South Pacific would be .... (comparative).
   Spending a week .... would be .... (superlative).
2 To grow up in a .... family would be .... (comparative).
   To grow up in a .... family would be .... (superlative).
3 Being a child in .... was .... (comparative).
   Being a child in .... was .... (superlative).
4 Living in .... would be .... (comparative).
   Living in .... would be .... (superlative).

b Pair Work Now practice the statements with a partner.

3 a Pair Work Use the structures you've practiced in this Language Focus to make statements about the following topics.

- growing up
- being a child
- being an adult

- living in a large city
- learning another language

b Pair Work Take turns having a conversation using as many of these sentences as you can.

- Seeing a good movie would be better than seeing a second-rate concert.
- Seeing the new movie at the Odeon would be the best thing that could happen this weekend.

"Well, I think that growing up in a happy, secure family is the most important thing."

"Well, the best thing about being a child was the fact that it didn't last long! I didn't really like being a kid."

Self-Check

COMMUNICATION CHALLENGE

PairWork Student A: Look at Challenge 11A on page 119. Student B: Look at Challenge 11B on page 120.

1 Write three new sentences or questions you learned.

....

....

....

2 a Review the language skills in this unit. In what situations might you use this language?

WHEN WOULD YOU USE THIS LANGUAGE?

	Situations
Ask for personal information	....
	....
	....
Express attitudes and opinions	....
	....
	....

b GroupWork Brainstorm ways to practice this language out of class. Imagine you are visiting an English-speaking country. Where/When might you need this language?

3 Out of Class Interview a group of friends or family members using the questions in Task Chain 1, Task 2. Bring the results of your interviews to the classroom and share them with the other students.

Question	Answer
1.	
2.	

4 Vocabulary check. Check [√] the words you know.

Adjectives/Adverbs

□ aggressive	□ hard-	□ patient
□ ambitious	working	□ personally
□ competitive	□ impatient	□ relaxed
□ earnest	□ inspiring	□ retired
□ easygoing	□ intense	□ tense
□ friendly	□ laid back	
□ fun-loving	□ lazy	

Nouns

□ achievement	□ choice	□ role model
□ ambition	□ graduation	□ scientist
□ anything	□ influence	□ vacation
□ career	□ ourselves	
□ childhood	□ resume	

Verbs

□ admire	□ expect	□ refuse
□ avoid	□ express	□ role play
□ complete	□ hang	□ share
□ consider	out	□ suggest
□ deny	□ hope	□ want
□ dislike	□ intend	

12 Attitudes

Warm-Up

Unit Goals

In this unit you will:

Speculate about future actions

"When my kids are grown they will have done all the things I only dreamed of."

Check and confirm facts and opinions

"You weren't really late for the interview, were you?"

"By this time next week I will have been to my last class of the semester."

1 a Look up these terms in your dictionary and then write definitions for them in your own words.

Leader: ....
Follower: ....
Advisor: ....

b GroupWork Discussion. Look at the pictures and find people who are leaders, followers, and advisors.

2 a Write one thing you plan to have achieved by . . .

- this time tomorrow. ....
- this time next week. ....
- this time next year. ....
- ten years from now. ....

b GroupWork Discussion. Share your responses with three or four other students. Who has the most interesting/unusual goals?

Task 1

a An optimist is someone who believes that things will turn out well. A pessimist believes that the worst will happen. Which of these expressions would be used by an optimist? Which would you expect to be used by a pessimist? Check [√] your answers.

	Optimist	*Pessimist*
▪ upbeat	☐	☐
▪ down in the dumps	☐	☐
▪ up-and-coming	☐	☐
▪ down side	☐	☐

b Use the expressions to complete these statements.

1 They say that she's an .... actress.
2 The .... of the job are the long hours I have to work.
3 She is .... about losing her job.
4 I'm feeling really .... about prospects for the new year.

Task 2

a These people were asked to react to the statement "In the future, things will not be as good as they are today." Write **O** if the person is *optimistic* and **P** if the person is *pessimistic*.

Picture 1

.... I disagree totally. The people I know look at conditions today with hope. They see a light. I think we're at a point where things are beginning to turn around. I feel upbeat. It's slowly getting better, and our children will be able to have a much better life than we have.

Picture 2

.... I agree. We see what is happening now, and we don't believe anything is going to get better—the economy, the environment— probably because of history. Things didn't seem to get better before, and most people don't think they're going to get better now.

Picture 3

.... We worry about everything in the world, but I think we're still optimistic. We worry about the worst times, but we always have the feeling that we'll be able to do better in the future. If things are bad now, we'll always recover. That's the feeling I have, anyway.

Picture 4

.... Do I see a negative attitude among people today? Yes, I do. It's because of a lack of leadership. People look to their leaders for direction, and they're not getting any. The politicians are not focused.

Source: Adapted from *USA Today*.

b 🎧 Listen to the tape and decide whether the speakers are optimistic or pessimistic. Write (O) or (P) in the chart.

PERSON	OPTIMIST (O)	PESSIMIST (P)	PICTURE NUMBER	KEYWORD(S)
Nicole				
Martin				
Rose				
Edgar				

c 🎧 Listen to the tape again and decide which of the people from Task 2 are talking. Write the picture number in the chart.

d 🎧 Listen once more. Which words gave you clues to the speakers' identities? Write the keywords in the chart.

Task 3

a How optimistic or pessimistic do you think you are? Put a check [√] mark in the appropriate box at left.

b Circle your answers to these questions.

1 What would you say? The bottle is . . .
half full.   half empty.

2 You are taking a trip. Do you assume that the flight will . . .
leave on time?   be delayed?

3 This time next year, do you think that you will be . . .
better off?   worse off?

4 Compared to you, do you think that your children will be . . .
better off?   worse off?

5 You lose your bag. Do you think that the person who finds it will . . .
return it to you?   keep it?

c Based on your answers, are you an optimist or a pessimist?

d Group Work Class discussion. Is the class basically optimistic or pessimistic?

Task 4

a Group Work Interview three other students. Ask them to agree or disagree with the statement: "In the future, things will not be as good as they are today." Make sure they give you a reason for their opinion. Decide whether they are optimists or pessimists.

b Group Work Discuss your findings as a class.

OPTIMIST

☐ 100%

☐ 75%

☐ 50%

☐ 25%

☐ 0%

☐ 25%

☐ 50%

☐ 75%

☐ 100%

PESSIMIST

"Hiroko agrees with the statement. She thinks that there will be fewer job opportunities for young people."

Language Focus 1 Future perfect

1 a Pair Work Practice. Take turns saying the first part of each statement. Your partner will complete it using one of the choices given.

1 By the time the kids get to be my age, the economy will have .... improved.   .... deteriorated.

2 By the end of this year, the world population will have .... doubled.   .... stabilized.

3 This time next year, they
.... will   .... won't
have discovered a cure for cancer.

4 Ten years from now, we'll all have been made
.... unemployed   .... wealthy
because of technology.

5 In the next few years, unemployment will have
.... risen.   fallen.

b From his/her answers, is your partner an optimist or a pessimist?

2 a Make some predictions.

1 This time next week, ...

2 By the end of this year, ...

3 This time next year, ...

4 By the turn of the century, ...

5 One hundred years from now, ...
....

b Pair Work Practice the statements with a partner.

c Group Work Tell another pair about your partner's predictions.

3 a Pair Work Interview your partner.

- time spent watching television per day? ....
- number of movies seen per month? ....
- time spent studying or reading per week? ....
- time spent traveling to work/school per week? ....
- money spent on food and drink per week? ....
- time spent talking on telephone per week? ....

b Now make statements about your partner.

"Anne says that by the turn of the century, the world population will have increased to ten billion."

"How much television do you watch a day?"

"By the end of the week you'll have watched 28 hours of television."

Task Chain 2 A born leader

Task 1

a Group Work Brainstorm. How many qualities can you think of that are associated with *leadership*? Add them to the diagram.

authority — organization — ....

Leadership — creativity

....

strength — .... — knowledge

b Now use the diagram to make as many statements about leaders as you can.

Example: Leaders are people who . . .

c Pair Work What kinds of leadership qualities are desirable in the following types of leaders? List them below.

1 the leader of an athletic organization ....
2 a religious or spiritual leader ....
3 a government leader ....
4 the head of a family ....
5 the head of a corporation ....

Task 2

These advertisement excerpts are from corporations and groups who want to hire people for the following leadership positions. Match the number of the ad to the position.

Positions

.... Coordinator of a new center to help immigrants in an inner city neighborhood

.... Chief conductor of a symphony orchestra

.... High school principal's assistant

.... Someone to take a group of young people on an outdoor adventure vacation in Canada

1 WE ARE LOOKING for a dynamic person with the right qualifications for this challenging new position. The successful applicant will be a leader who is sensitive to people from many different cultures, who can work with people of all ages, and who is totally committed to equal opportunity for all peoples.

2 We are looking for a strong but caring leader to take our group in new directions. In addition to creative and artistic skills, you will need to be able to turn a very talented but diverse group of people into a team. You must also be prepared to travel.

3 WANTED Caring individual, with leadership potential who is comfortable in the great outdoors. Must like travelling and working with young people. May involve long hours and limited budget.

4 Do you have good organizational skills? Do you have experience in an educational environment? Do you like working with young people? If so, then you may be the person we are looking for.

Task 3

a 🎧 Listen to the conversation. Who is speaking? Who are they discussing?

b 🎧 Listen again and note what is said about each person. Write a (+) for a positive evaluation, and a (–) for a negative evaluation.

	Angela	*Marty*
• As a team member, not leader	....	....
• Self-motivation	....	....
• Ability to delegate	....	....
• Attitude toward criticism	....	....
• Attitude toward people from other cultures	....	....

c PairWork Discussion. Who do you think is the best person for the leadership position?

Task 4

You choose: Do Ⓐ or Ⓑ.

Ⓐ People play different roles in different situations. Think of the different roles you play in these situations, and fill in the chart with the appropriate number (1 = often; 2 = sometimes; 3 = seldom; 4 = never).

"Well, I'm rarely leader at home, because I'm always being told what to do by the rest of my family."

	AT HOME	AT WORK	AT SCHOOL	WITH FRIENDS
leader				
follower				
planner				
adviser				

GroupWork Compare responses and talk about them.

Ⓑ Make a list of good leaders you have known. What makes each person a good leader?

GroupWork Compare lists, then make a single list of essential leadership qualities.

Language Focus 2 Tag questions

A You have to travel a lot in your job, don't you?

B Yes, I do.

or

B Well, no, I don't, as a matter of fact.

1 a Are these speakers expecting a *yes* or *no* answer? Circle your choice.

  1 "You have to travel a lot in your job, don't you?"   **Yes No**

  2 "She hasn't demonstrated many leadership qualities, has she?"   **Yes No**

  3 "She has never extended herself at work, has she?"   **Yes No**

  4 "He should have given more detailed answers, shouldn't he?"   **Yes No**

  5 "You were in school with my sister, weren't you?"   **Yes No**

  6 "I guess we've applied for the same position, haven't we?"   **Yes No**

  b **Pair Work** Practice with another student. Give answers following the model at left.

2 a Match the questions and answers.

Questions
1 You weren't really late for the interview, were you?
2 They've always had leadership potential, haven't they?
3 You should have said you'd be away tomorrow, shouldn't you?
4 They haven't gotten used to your style already, have they?
5 Yes, it was a tough interview, but it was also a valuable experience, wasn't it?

Answers
.... I did. Unfortunately, the message got lost in the system.
.... Yes. Everything I do seems predictable these days.
.... Yes. I learned a lot from it, I guess.
.... Only a few minutes, but they weren't ready for me, anyway.
.... No. It's something they developed during the training program.

  b **Pair Work** Think of your own answers, and practice asking and answering the questions with a partner.

A You weren't particularly late for the interview, were you?

B Yes, I was, actually. I got off at the wrong subway stop and had to walk further than I'd anticipated.

3 Complete the following statements with appropriate tags.

  1 "You should have called, ... ?"
  2 "You've been a group leader before, ... ?"
  3 "You've never considered yourself more of a follower than a leader, ... ?"
  4 "Most of the students in the class seem self-motivated, ... ?"
  5 "Most people have a healthy attitude towards people from other cultures, ... ?"
  6 "We'd all rather cooperate than compete, ... ?

Self-Check

COMMUNICATION CHALLENGE

Pair Work Student A: Look at Challenge 12A on page 122. Student B: Look at Challenge 12B on page 124.

1 Write three new sentences or questions you learned.

....

....

....

2 Review the language skills you practiced in this unit. In what situations might you use this language?

WHEN WOULD YOU USE THIS LANGUAGE?

	Situations
Speculate about future actions	....
	....
	....
Check and confirm facts and opinions	....
	....
	....

3 Out of Class Talk to a friend or relative about the people they work with or go to school with. Make a list of the qualities they admire and dislike in other people. Report back to the class and make a single list. What similarities/differences are there in what people reported?

GOOD QUALITIES	BAD QUALITIES

4 Vocabulary check. Check [√] the words you know.

Adjectives/Adverbs

- ☐ caring
- ☐ challenging
- ☐ consistent
- ☐ constructive
- ☐ detailed
- ☐ dynamic
- ☐ hopeful
- ☐ limited
- ☐ multicultural
- ☐ negative
- ☐ optimistic
- ☐ particularly
- ☐ pessimistic
- ☐ potential
- ☐ prepared
- ☐ talented
- ☐ upbeat

Nouns

- ☐ applicant
- ☐ attitude
- ☐ authority
- ☐ conditions
- ☐ creativity
- ☐ economy
- ☐ equal opportunity
- ☐ evaluation
- ☐ hope
- ☐ job opportunity
- ☐ knowledge
- ☐ leadership
- ☐ optimist
- ☐ orchestra
- ☐ organization
- ☐ pessimist
- ☐ principal
- ☐ strength
- ☐ talent

Verbs

- ☐ agree
- ☐ delegate
- ☐ demonstrate
- ☐ disagree
- ☐ extend
- ☐ speculate

13 Time For a Change

Warm-Up

Unit Goals

In this unit you will:

Express past and future expectations

"We were supposed to have gone to Yani's party last weekend."

"I'm supposed to sign up for the new aerobics class by Friday."

Describe interesting and significant events in the past

"Well, I spent a year in Brazil as an exchange student."

1 Look at the person in the pictures. What significant events are occurring in his life?

2 a Group Work Discussion. Talk about significant things that have happened to you in these categories:

- education
- travel
- employment
- relationships

b Group Work In what ways did these events change your life?

c Group Work What things do you expect to happen to you in the next few years in these areas of your life?

3 a Group Work Discussion. Do you . . .

- get up at the same time every day?
- have the same thing for breakfast every day?
- hang out with the same people most of the time?
- watch the same shows on television every week?
- wear the same kind of clothing most of the time?
- do the same kinds of exercise all the time?

b Group Work Compare your responses with three or four other students. How predictable are you? Who is the most/least predictable person in the group?

Task Chain 1 Changing times

Task 1

a Pair Work Look at the pictures. When do you think they were taken? What differences do you see among the pictures?

Picture 1

Picture 2

Picture 3

b What do you think were the major changes experienced by the people in the first two pictures as they grew up? Make notes in the blank lines below. Over the next 20 years, what do you think will be the major changes experienced by the children in the third picture?

Picture 1 ....

....

Picture 2 ....

....

Picture 3 ....

....

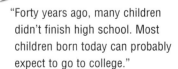

"Forty years ago, many children didn't finish high school. Most children born today can probably expect to go to college."

LEARNING STRATEGY

Selective listening = listening for the most important words and information.

c What did children born forty years ago expect for their future? What do children born now expect? What differences do you think there are? Make notes in the chart and discuss your ideas.

	40 YEARS AGO	NOW
education		
health		
employment		
leisure		

where
ou're invited . . . go to the movies!
meet me for lunch
what do you do?
why
s my family
neighborhood

Task 2

a 🎧 Listen. You will hear two of the people in the pictures from Task 1 talking about their lives. Try to guess when each speaker was born and what they are talking about.

Speaker 1 was born .... years ago. Topic: ....

Speaker 2 was born .... years ago. Topic: ....

b 🎧 Listen again to the first speaker and list all the differences he notes between his life as a young adult and his life now.

Then	*Now*
....	....
....	....
....	....
....	....
....	....

"Well, the most significant event was meeting her boyfriend—that happened a year ago."

c 🎧 Listen again to the second speaker and note the significant events.

Event	*When*
1	....
2	....
3	....
4	....
5	....

d **Group Work** Work with two other students to decide when these events occurred.

Task 3

a What are the differences between your life now and 5, 10, and 15 years ago? Fill in the chart.

	5 YEARS AGO	10 YEARS AGO	15 YEARS AGO
work			
relationships			
living arrangements			
education			

"Well, fifteen years ago, I was a child living at home and totally dependent on my parents. Today, I share an apartment with my brother. Ten years ago, I was just starting high school, whereas today I have a college diploma."

b **Group Work** Discuss your responses.

Language Focus 1 Review of past & perfect tenses

Dear Deb,

Please help me. I (1) .... (have) terrible problems with my parents recently. They just don't understand me. I'm almost an adult, but they simply don't seem to realize that I (2) .... (grow up), and they continue to treat me as though I were a child. I've never been allowed to stay out after nine o'clock at night. Last week I (3) .... (come) in at nine thirty, and they said that I wasn't allowed out for the next month because they (4) .... (be) so worried. I (5) .... (play) cards at my friend's house next door. Now, the big problem is that I (6) .... (see) this guy at school for a few months. My parents don't know of course—they wouldn't approve, but I really like him. Anyway, I (7) .... (talk) with him on the phone the other day, and he asked me to come to his parents' anniversary party next Saturday night. But I can't go because I'm grounded! What should I do?

1 a Read the following letter and put the verbs in parentheses into the appropriate tense.

b Identify the tenses in the blanks by writing the number in the chart.

TENSE	BLANK
simple past	
present perfect	
past perfect	
present perfect progressive	
past perfect progressive	

2 a Answer the following questions, giving as many details as you can.

1 When did you first use English outside of the classroom?

....

2 Has anyone ever spoken to you in English outside of the classroom?

....

3 How long have you been learning English?

....

4 Had you studied any other languages before learning English?

....

"I studied Portuguese for two years before learning English."

b Now think of three additional questions and interview two other students.

1 .... ?

2 .... ?

3 .... ?

3 a Think of some dramatic or important event in your life. Make notes using as many of the past and perfect tense forms as you can.

b **Group Work** Take turns telling your story. Your partners will note the different tense forms they hear.

"Well, I'll definitely reduce the amount of TV I watch. I might try changing my workout. But I would definitely never take a healthful vacation."

Task 1

a 🎧 **Group Work** Listen. What is wrong with Barbara? What does her friend offer to do? What do you think being in a "rut" means?

b **Group Work** Are you in a rut? Brainstorm ways of changing your daily routine.

Task 2

a Skim the following article and add these subheadings in the blanks:

Personal Development   **Career Changes**   **At Leisure**
Family and Community   **Better Health**

b Read the article again and decide which of these things you will definitely/might/would never do to get out of a rut.

c **Group Work** Discuss your responses with three or four other students.

The Same Old Life: Getting Yourself Out of a Rut

You've eaten the same thing for breakfast every day for three years, then taken the same car pool to the same job. Your life is more of the same after work. It's time to get out of your rut. Making any of the following small changes can lead to big changes in your life.

....

- Learn a new job skill. Pick something you have always wanted to do, such as learning a new computer program. Take a class at a community college.
- Earn that college degree. Study a course catalog to determine what it takes to get started. Or earn a certificate given by the professional association in your field. Inform your supervisor about your goal.
- Subscribe to a professional or career journal in your field. If you already subscribe to one, write an article or letter to the editor.

....

- Reduce the amount of time you spend watching television by an hour a day. Use the extra time for something special, such as reading a book or doing a hobby.
- Start a family project, such as planning your next vacation or planting a backyard garden.
- Fulfill a fantasy. For example, take dancing lessons, or join a neighborhood chess club or sports team.

....

- Take a walk. Use your lunch break to explore the neighborhood near your workplace.
- Vary your workout. Add new challenges by making your workout more interesting.
- Explore a new cuisine. Sample local ethnic restaurants or learn to make new dishes.
- Take a healthful vacation. Attend a sports camp or sign up for a bike tour of a national park.

....

- Play "tourist" in your own town. Check out a guidebook or ask your visitor's bureau for information on local tourist attractions.
- Take your camera with you on daily activities. Look for scenes that would make interesting pictures.
- Write a letter to someone you haven't heard from in a while. It might revive a friendship.

....

- Ask your children, spouse, or friends to suggest their favorite things to do, then join in—enthusiastically.
- Volunteer. A nearby hospital, library, or theater group could probably use your help. Start by committing yourself to a single event or project. If you enjoy the work, you can build a long-term relationship.

Source: *Vitality*, June 1994.

my name is
exercise!
hello
how are you?
where do you live?
my sister

	STUDENT 1			STUDENT 2			STUDENT 3		
	yes	maybe	no	yes	maybe	no	yes	maybe	no
Learn a new job skill	☐	☐	☐	☐	☐	☐	☐	☐	☐
....	☐	☐	☐	☐	☐	☐	☐	☐	☐
....	☐	☐	☐	☐	☐	☐	☐	☐	☐
....	☐	☐	☐	☐	☐	☐	☐	☐	☐
....	☐	☐	☐	☐	☐	☐	☐	☐	☐
....	☐	☐	☐	☐	☐	☐	☐	☐	☐
....	☐	☐	☐	☐	☐	☐	☐	☐	☐

Task 3

a **Pair Work** Create a survey to find out how other students would get out of a rut. Add your own ideas or use the suggestions from the article.

b **Group Work** Interview three other students to find out if they would use these ideas to get out of a rut. Now compare results with your partner.

A If you were in a rut, would you learn a new job skill?

B You must be kidding—change one rut for another?

Task 4

In Task 1, you heard Barbara talking about being in a rut. Her friend gave her a copy of the article from Task 2, and is now asking her about what changes she made. Listen to the plans she made, and the results. Make notes in the chart

	PLAN	RESULT
Career		
Personal development		
Health		
Leisure		
Family/community		

Task 5

a Think of three things about your lifestyle that you would like to change and write them in the first column.

WHAT I PLAN TO CHANGE	HOW I PLAN TO CHANGE
1	
2	
3	

b **Pair Work** Work together to make a plan to change. Write your plans in the second column.

c **Group Work** Compare plans with another pair.

A I'd like to make some new friends.

B Why don't you join a club?

Language Focus 2 *Supposed to*

1 Which of the following refer to past events and which to future events? Write P for past events and F for future expectations in the blank next to each sentence.

.... I'm supposed to enroll in the new computer course by Friday.

.... They were supposed to have sent me the enrollment form in the mail.

.... We were supposed to have completed the assignment by the end of semester.

.... The survey is supposed to be published by the end of the week.

.... The interviewer was supposed to have asked more detailed questions.

.... They are supposed to provide the information in time for next weekend's newspapers.

2 Complete the following statements.

a Barbara was supposed to have learned a new wordprocessing program, but ....

b She was supposed to have taken up painting, but ....
....

c She .... , but she twisted her ankle.

d She was supposed to have taken a tour of the city, but ....
....

e She .... , but she had no librarian training.

3 a Think of ways to complete these statements.

1 The teacher was supposed to have given us an exam yesterday, but
....

2 We were supposed to have prepared for the exam, but ....
....

3 They are supposed to come to the party, but ....

4 We are supposed to finish the assignment by Monday, but ....
....

5 The teacher was supposed to have handed our last assignment back to us by Friday, but ....

b Group Work Compare responses. Who has the most interesting or unusual responses?

"Adriana was supposed to have called her parents last week, but she forgot."

4 a Pair Work Find out three things that your partner was supposed to have done in the last month, but didn't do.

b Group Work Report what your partner said to another pair.

c Pair Work Write down three things you are supposed to do by the end of the year and then tell another student.

Self-Check

COMMUNICATION CHALLENGE

Group Work Look at Challenge 13 on page 126.

1 Write three new sentences or questions you learned.

....

....

....

2 a Review the language skills you practiced in this unit. In what situations might you use this language?

WHEN WOULD YOU USE THIS LANGUAGE?

	Situations
Express past and future expectations	....
	....
Describe interesting and significant events in the past	....

b Group Work Brainstorm ways to practice this language out of class. Imagine you are visiting an English-speaking country. Where/When might you need this language?

3 Out of Class Find someone who has an interesting or dramatic story to tell. Make notes, and then retell the story in class. Who has the most interesting or most dramatic story?

Name	Story Events
1.	
2.	

4 Vocabulary check. Check [√] the words you know.

Adjectives/Adverbs			Nouns			Verbs		
☐ dependent	☐ main	☐ significant	☐ catalog	☐ expectations	☐ supervisor	☐ approve	☐ happen	☐ sample
☐ ethnic	☐ predictable	☐ totally	☐ car pool	☐ leisure	☐ workout	☐ break out	☐ help	☐ subscribe
☐ ever	☐ professional		☐ change	☐ relationships		☐ change	☐ note	☐ understand
☐ first	☐ selective		☐ difference	☐ rut		☐ experience	☐ occur	☐ vary

14 They're Only Words

Unit Goals

In this unit you will:

Talk about cultural attitudes and beliefs

"In some cultures, it is considered unlucky to keep certain kinds of animals as pets."

Express a point of view

"People who paint graffiti are destructive vandals who ought to be punished."

Warm-Up

Picture 1

Picture 2

Picture 3

Picture 4

Picture 5

1 Look at the pictures. Where would you see these notices? Write the number of the picture in the correct blank.

....

Customers may have a fit upstairs.

....

Our wines leave nothing to hope for.

....

Guests are expected to complain to the manager between the hours of 9 and 11 A.M. daily.

....

Please do not feed the animals. If you have food, please give it to the guard on duty.

....

We take your bags and send them in all directions.

2 What is wrong with the notices? Correct them.

Task Chain 1 The magic of language

Task 1

a PairWork Discussion. In this chain you will use the words *taboo* and *euphemism*. Look at these definitions and decide what the words have in common.

> **taboo** *n.* **1** an act or subject that religion or society dissaproves of strongly: *There is a taboo against couples living together before marriage in many societies.* **2** an agreement not to discuss (touch, do, etc.) s.t. *-adj.* under a taboo: *It is taboo to use bad words in front of my parents.*
>
> **euphemism** *n.* **1** a more pleasant word or description used to replace a word or description that is considered unpleasant: *To say, "heavy" is a euphemism for "fat". -adj.* **euphemistic**.

From *The Newbury House Dictionary of American English.*

b Does your language have taboo words or euphemisms? What happens when people use these words? Have some taboo words become more acceptable in recent years?

Task 2

a 🎧 Listen to the anthropologist talking about taboos in different societies. What taboos are mentioned? Listen and fill in the blanks under "taboo".

TABOO	SOCIETY
supernatural, sex, death	
	Zuni Indians in New Mexico
use of word "bull"	
	Aborigines in Australia

b 🎧 Now listen again for the societies where these things are taboo. Fill in the blanks under "society".

c What are some of the euphemisms for *death*?

d PairWork Imagine you are the interviewer. What questions would you like to ask the anthropologist?

Task 3

a Pair Work Discussion. Skim the following text. How would you describe the tone? Check [√] one.

☐ humorous   ☐ serious   ☐ sarcastic   ☐ academic

Have you noticed how the English language is changing from under our very tongues? We don't throw trash out of our homes any more but dispose of "recyclable products." This obsession for creating euphemisms is even extending to the world of employment.

The other day, *The Southern Express* ran an advertisement for a firm looking for a Leathergoods Maintenance Officer: Footwear Division. What on earth would such a person do? Why, shine shoes, of course. Because the term "shoeshine boy" is no longer politically correct (and who wants to shine shoes anyway, even one's own?), the person who wrote the advertisement came up with a nice euphemism. Of course, the person who gets the job will still end up shining shoes.

The same firm is also looking for a Sanitary Engineer: Personnel Services. Such a person used to be called a Washroom Attendant, someone who hands out towels and cleans up the messy public washroom. However, providing a personal service is much more dignified than attending to other people's messy habits.

And employers aren't the only ones who are experts at creating euphemisms. Recently, one well-known journalist was accused of lying. He denied the accusation, but admitted that he might have been economical with the truth. A politician accused of being drunk at a public function also denied the charge, saying that he had been tired and emotional.

What do these examples tell us? Well, they either indicate that as a language English is alive and well, or that it is about to pass away.

ORIGINAL TERM	EUPHEMISM
to lie	
trash	
to be drunk	

b What euphemisms does the article use for the following terms?

c Which professions does the article name as using euphemisms?

Task 4

a Pair Work What do you think the following expressions mean?

"to pass away" ....
"to carry a few extra pounds" ....
"to have a preowned car" ....
"to be temporarily embarrassed for money" ....
"to depart from the truth" ....

b Group Work Compare your responses with another pair's responses.

c Pair Work Think of euphemisms for the following jobs and compare your euphemism with another person.

Cleaner   Street-corner vendor   Hotel doorperson
Waiter   Security guard

"Well, we think that 'to pass away' means 'to die'."

Language Focus 1 Complex passives

1 a Match column 1 with column 2 to complete the statements.

Column 1
1 In our super-sophisticated society,
2 In many different societies,
3 Among some Australian aboriginal tribes,
4 Among the Zuni Indians of New Mexico,
5 In parts of the United States,

Column 2
.... it is believed that a person's name should never be used.
.... it is considered unlucky to mention animal names.
.... it is considered improper to use the word "bull".
.... it is believed that certain subjects are unlucky.
.... it is prohibited to use the word for "frogs".

b 🎧 Listen to the tape and check your answers.

2 Pair Work Make statements following the model at left.

a In some places, people believe that words have magic properties.
b In some Australian aboriginal tribes, members have public and private names.
c In ancient times, people thought that language could cure sickness and disease.
d People sometimes assume that changing the name of a place will bring good luck.

"In most societies, people believe it is unlucky to talk about death."

"In most societies, it is believed unlucky to talk about death."

3 a Pair Work Student A plays the part of an interviewer. Student B plays the part of a famous anthropologist. Ask and answer questions using these cues.

A: Are taboos only found in primitive societies?
B: No / sophisticated societies / believed / certain subjects are unlucky
A: Can you give examples of animal taboos?
B: New Mexico / believed / bad / mention / word for frogs
A: What is the most extraordinary taboo you know of?
B: Among Australian Aborigines / prohibited for / person's name / be mentioned
A: What happens if taboos are broken?
B: in many societies / not unusual / people / be severely punished

b Now change roles and do the task again.

"In our society, it is considered a taboo to mention . . ."

4 Group Work Think of three taboos in your country. Take turns making statements about them, using the model at left.

Task 1

a 🎧 You will hear a disagreement between two people. They are arguing over an incident that was reported in the newspaper with this headline. Can you predict what the argument is about?

The Town Crier

Four-Month Suspended Sentence for Spray-Can Kid

b 🎧 Listen and make a note of the arguments for and against the graffiti artist.

ARGUMENTS FOR	ARGUMENTS AGAINST

c Which of the pieces of graffiti pictured did Dennis Wilson paint?

Picture 1

Picture 2

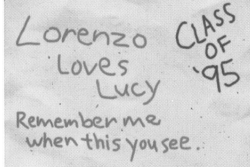

Letter 1

Dear Madam,

I write to express my disgust at the rather weak-minded attitude taken by your newspaper towards the sentence given to a certain Dennis Wilson. We expect the press to uphold the law, not to undermine it. I do not know the young man, but I believe he has been in trouble more than once before. Perhaps this will teach him a lesson he won't forget.

Letter 2

Dear Editor,

I was encouraged by the attitude taken by your newspaper on the matter of young Dennis Wilson. Far from being the menace that some people say he is, Dennis is a responsible, though high-spirited youth who is well known in the neighborhood. As he said to the judge, he was only trying to brighten up the neighborhood with a "mural". I must say that I enjoy looking at the mural as I walk to work in the morning.

Letter 3

To the Editor:

I was disappointed at the harsh and unfair reactions of much of the community in the case of Dennis Wilson. The boy is creative and gifted, and the work of art which he has produced is a major improvement to what was an ugly wall. To call it graffiti is absurd. It might look a little strange to those people who do not appreciate modern art, but surely even they would rather look at a colorful wall than a dirty concrete one. I believe that the judge in this case made a mistake, and I would like to take this opportunity of congratulating you for pointing this out.

Letter 4

Editor:

I wish to cancel my subscription to your newspaper. The attitude you took to the Wilson case has totally destroyed your credibility as far as I am concerned. Your role is to report the facts objectively, not to express opinions. As far as I am concerned, that boy got off too lightly. He's a menace to himself and all of those around him.

Task 2

a Here are some letters to the local paper about the Wilson incident. Which letters are for and which against the graffiti artist?

b Which letter was written by one of the speakers in Task 1? Give reasons for your choice.

c Write a letter to the newspaper expressing your point of view.

- How can you say such a thing?
- Oh, come on.
- I disagree.
- I'm afraid I just can't understand your attitude.

Task 3

a Pair Work Decide what you think should happen to Dennis Wilson. Take opposing sides. Use the expressions in the model at left.

b Pair Work Change partners and roles and do the task again.

Task 4

a Group Work Discussion. What would you do if you saw some people spraying graffiti on a wall? Make a list of options.

b Group Work Compare options with another group.

Language Focus 2 Idioms

1 a Look at the following idioms (in italics) and match them with their meanings.

Idioms

1 My friends enjoyed the speeches at the political rally, but I thought that they were *a lot of hot air.*
2 I'm *having second thoughts* about going out with Lucio because he never has any money.
3 Ron really *put his foot in his mouth* when he let on about the surprise party for Nick.
4 Naomi's really been *throwing her weight around* since she got that promotion.
5 Renata's been so down since her boyfriend left that I finally had to tell her to *snap out of it.*
6 My brother *hit it off* so well with his new girlfriend that they decided to get married after dating for only a month.
7 I had to *bite my tongue* when the boss started telling those tasteless jokes.
8 After listening to the front office staff gossiping about everyone else in the office, I finally had to *give them a piece of my mind.*

Meaning

.... to consider changing one's mind
.... to speak severely to someone over whom you have authority
.... to say something extremely indiscrete
.... to speak a lot, but in a way that makes very little sense
.... to use one's authority
.... to make an effort to overcome negative feelings
.... to get along well with someone on first meeting them
.... to keep silent when you really want to speak

"Ron really said something stupid when he let on about the surprise party for Nick."

b Now rewrite the statements using the example on the left.

c Pair Work Compare statements with another student.

2 a Pair Work Match the following questions/statements and responses and practice them.

Questions/Statements
1 How was your date?
2 What did you think when you heard the news?
3 I've decided to marry Mickey.
4 When do you want to get together?
5 What did you do when he asked for help?

Responses
.... You must be out of your mind.
.... I bent over backwards, but it didn't make any difference.
.... I don't know. Just get in touch.
.... I couldn't believe my ears.
.... He turned out to be a real pain in the neck.

b Pair Work Take turns making statements or asking questions. Use the above responses to your partner's statements or questions.

Self-Check

COMMUNICATION CHALLENGE

Group Work Work in two groups. Group A: Look at Challenge 14A on page 125. Group B: Look at Challenge 14B on page 127.

1 Write three new sentences or questions you learned.

....

....

....

2 Review the language skills you practiced in this unit. In what situations might you use this language?

WHEN WOULD YOU USE THIS LANGUAGE?

	Situations
Talk about cultural attitudes and beliefs	....
	....
Express a point of view	....
	....

3 **Out of Class** Find examples of graffiti, slogans, etc. in your neighborhood. Bring them to class and be prepared to discuss them in English. Alternative: If possible, bring photographs of "street art" to class and discuss them. Do they have any value or not?

EXAMPLE OF GRAFFITI	DOES IT HAVE VALUE?	
	YES	NO

4 Vocabulary check. Check [√] the words you know.

Adjectives/Adverbs

☐ aboriginal	☐ destructive	☐ sarcastic
☐ academic	☐ fake	☐ serious
☐ artificial	☐ high-spirited	☐ sophisticated
☐ certain	☐ lightly	☐ temporary
☐ clever	☐ magical	☐ terminal
☐ considered	☐ religious	☐ unlucky

Nouns

☐ credibility	☐ mural	☐ spray can
☐ euphemism	☐ options	☐ supernatural
☐ graffiti	☐ origins	☐ taboo
magic	☐ popularity	☐ vandal
☐ marketer	☐ sale	

Verbs

☐ cancel	☐ express	☐ turn off
☐ check	☐ mention	☐ uphold
☐ cooperate	☐ prohibit	
☐ cure	☐ punish	

Task 1

Pretend that you are one of these people. Make up a story surrounding the pictures. Think about these questions and make notes.

1 Where did it take place?
2 Who were your companions?
3 What was the most frightening thing about the whole incident?
4 How did your companions react?
5 What did you expect was going to happen?
6 What happened immediately after the incident pictured happened?
7 What did you suggest doing?
8 What were you supposed to have done that would have prevented the incident?

Task 2

a Classify these words.

| suggest | intend | remind | want | ask |
| consider | demand | expect | hope | deny |

WORDS TO DESCRIBE MENTAL STATES	WORDS TO REPORT WHAT SOMEONE SAYS

b Fill in the blanks with the most appropriate word from the chart.

1 What languages other than English would you .... learning if you had the choice?
2 What do you .... we do after class?
3 What do you .... to do during the next vacation?
4 What would you most like to .... the teacher about his/her personal life?
5 As a child, what did you most .... to be when you grew up?
6 .... ?
7 .... ?
8 .... ?

c PairWork Add three questions of your own using words from the list, and take turns asking and answering questions.

Task 3

a 🎧 Listen. You will hear two people answering five questions. Make a note of their responses.

Questions	Di	Steve
1 .... ?	....	....
2 .... ?	....	....
3 .... ?	....	....
4 .... ?	....	....
5 .... ?	....	....

b PairWork Study the responses and guess what the questions were. Write the questions in the blank lines above.

c GroupWork Take turns asking each other these questions. One person records the answers and reports them to the class.

Communication Challenges

Challenge 1

a **PairWork** Imagine that your school is 100 years old this year. Plan a week-long festival to celebrate the event. Decide when it will be held, who will be invited, what events will be staged. Now write a program.

b **GroupWork** Work with another pair and ask them about their festival program.

c **GroupWork** Put the programs on the classroom walls. Circulate and decide which group has the best program.

d Take turns telling the rest of the class about your festival and inviting them to come.

Back to School Week! Come Celebrate With Us!

Atlas School is One Hundred Years Old This Week!

 MONDAY
Evening Celebration Concert: Hear the Atlas School Symphony Orchestra conducted by Akron Symphony Orchestra's Maestro Steven Challenor, one of our most famous graduates.

 TUESDAY
Gala Track Meet: Show your prowess in track and field events at this very special all-day sporting carnival. Meet Gloria Day, 200 meter Olympic sprint champion.

 WEDNESDAY
Honor our oldest alumni at a special afternoon tea ceremony. The guest of honor will be celebrated 95-year-old author Jack Richards.

 THURSDAY
On Thursday evening, join the Board of Governors and distinguished guests at the opening of the new Access Learning Center.

 FRIDAY
Quiz Night! Get a group of friends together and test your general knowledge. There will be great prizes for the winning teams.

SATURDAY/SUNDAY
All the fun of the fair! Help the week go out with a bang with two days of fun, music, competitions, and prizes at the Grand Finale Fair.

Challenge 2A

Task 1

Student A

a You are a journalist. You are interviewing two people together, one who was lost for several days on a remote island and the person who found him/her. You are going to write a story about the incident, and need to know the following information:

- how he/she got lost
- how he/she felt while he/she was lost
- what he/she ate and drank
- how long he/she was lost
- what things happened to him/her
- how he/she was found
- how he/she felt when he/she was found

b Interview the person who was lost, and then the person who found him/her. Ask questions and make a note of similarities and differences in the facts and opinions of the two people.

Task 2

Now use your notes to tell the story to another group.

Challenge 3

A I'd take classes in ceramics.

B I had no idea you were interested in ceramics.

A I'm not, but it's such a boring hobby, there must be lots of interesting conversations in the class.

B That's a crazy idea. I'd find out about the place before I go. I'd check the encyclopedia and I'd visit the local consulate. They always have lots of information.

a Pair Work You've just moved, or are about to move, to another country to start a position as a computer programmer with a large company. You know very little about this country. Brainstorm ideas for meeting people and finding out about your new country.

b Group Work Work with another pair, and write down ten ideas. Rank the ideas from most to least interesting (1 = most interesting). Now rank them again from most to least practical (1 = most practical).

IDEAS		INTERESTING	PRACTICAL
1			
2			
3			
4			
5			
6			
7			
8			
9			
10			

c Group Work Compare lists. Which pair has the most interesting ideas overall?

d where
you're invited ... go to the movies! meet me for lunc
what do you do?
is my family why
neighborhood

Challenge 4

a Listen to four people talking about someone they live with and make a list of the individuals' positive and negative points.

b **Pair Work** Decide which of the people you would like to live with and which you would not like to live with.

Challenge 6A

"I asked if they could put the CDs back in their cases and then put them on the bookshelf."

This is your room after a Friday night party. Your roommate is returning from a vacation the following day. Some of your friends say that they will stay and clean up because you're going away for the weekend, and you want the room fixed before your roommate returns. You give them a note with the following instructions. Call your roommate and ask if your instructions were carried out. Tell him/her what you wanted done.

CDs back in cases on bookshelf
bottles and glasses in garbage bags
plates in garbage bags
marks cleaned off wall
rugs straightened out
books back in bookcase
paintings hung back on wall
potted plant picked up and put on balcony
chairs put around table
CD player plugged in and put on desk

Challenge 2B

Student B

You have just been rescued from a remote island, and are talking to a journalist who wants to know what happened. Also present is the person who rescued you.

You were flying your light plane off the coast when the engine failed. You managed to land on the beach of an uninhabited island. Amazingly, you were not hurt. Think about how you felt when the accident happened, and what you ate and drank. You walked into the center of the island and slept in a cave. You were there for about a week. One night, you had a dream in which a friend told you to walk back to the coast. You did so, and when you got there you saw a boat. You lit a fire, and the person on the boat saw the fire and rescued you. Think about how you felt when you were rescued.

Key to Warm-up Quiz (page 51)

(Answers are in boldface.)

Question 1: The dodo is **(a) an extinct animal** (b) a make believe creature (c) a living animal
Question 2: The giant panda is an endangered animal. **True** or false.
Question 3: Kangaroos are considered gourmet food in Australia. True or **false.**
Question 4: Elephants are used as working animals in **(a) Thailand** (b) Singapore (c) Taiwan.
Question 5: Kiwis are (a) small horses **(b) birds** (c) make believe creatures
Question 6: Elderly people who have pets tend to live longer than those who live alone. **True** or false?

Task 1

a You want to go on an eco-tourism trip, so you picked up a couple of brochures. Now you have to decide which of these trips would be best to take. You go to see a travel agent who has more information about each trip.

b Ask the travel agent questions to find out which trip . . .

- is the most exciting.
- is the most dangerous.
- lets you see the most exotic animals.
- lets you see the most endangered species.
- takes you to the most mysterious places.
- has the most extreme weather.
- is the most unusual.
- is the cheapest.

c Ask any other questions you like and decide which trip you are going to take, and why.

15-DAY TRIP TO THE SOUTH POLE

Take the trip of a lifetime! A never-to-be-forgotten journey to the frozen wastelands of the South Pole. Available to specially-selected clients only.

21-DAY ECO-TRIP TO THE AMAZON JUNGLE

Travel the Amazon River. See beautiful and exotic creatures and experience the mystery of the jungle.

TWO-WEEK TRIP TO NORTHERN AUSTRALIA

Visit the jungles of Far North Queensland. See some of the most unusual creatures on earth in their native habitat.

Task 2

Now change roles and do the task again.

Challenge 2C

Student C

You are taking part in an interview between a journalist and a person you rescued from an island. You were on a sailing trip when you saw the wreckage of a light plane in the water. You had heard on the news that the plane had been missing for four days. You went ashore and found the person who looked frightened and confused. He/She had had nothing to eat or drink and had not slept while on the island.

Challenge 6B

You've just returned from a vacation and you receive a call from your roommate who had a party while you were away. He/She asked his/her friends to clean up after the party because he/she had to go away for the weekend. Listen to what the friends were asked to do and then say what they really did.

"Well, the CDs have been put back in their cases, but they've been put on the desk, not on the bookcase."

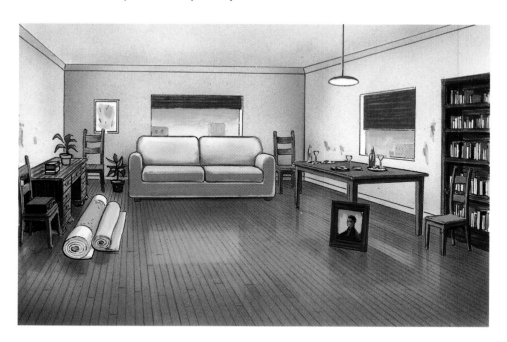

you're invited... to the movies! meet me for lunch
what do you do?
my family why neighborhood

Challenge 7B

Task 1

You are a travel agent. A customer comes in with several brochures. You look up the following additional information to help him/her decide which trip to take. Be prepared to answer other questions as well.

Task 2

Now change roles and do the task again.

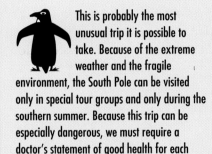

15-DAY TRIP TO THE SOUTH POLE

This is probably the most unusual trip it is possible to take. Because of the extreme weather and the fragile environment, the South Pole can be visited only in special tour groups and only during the southern summer. Because this trip can be especially dangerous, we must require a doctor's statement of good health for each client. It isn't cheap, but it's unique.

21-DAY ECO-TRIP TO THE AMAZON JUNGLE

This boat trip is probably the most exciting one we offer. Clients travel to the mysterious upper reaches of the Amazon River, where they see the most exotic wildlife on earth. Travel in the jungle can be dangerous, although we haven't lost a client yet! The trip is reasonably priced.

TWO-WEEK TRIP TO NORTHERN AUSTRALIA

This trip is a must for clients who are interested in wildlife. They will have a chance to see many unusual and endangered species including the extremely rare Northern Tree Kangaroo. The great distances make this one of the more expensive trips we offer.

Challenge 8A

* image of company should be dignified
* wants to appeal to people with good taste
* doesn't want to spend too much on the advertising campaign
* need to develop a product range that can be worn in both casual and formal situations

Task 1

Student A

Work with Students B and C to design a corporate image, including a logo and slogan for a clothing company. Use the following notes which you made while interviewing the Managing Director.

Task 2

Student B

When you have finished, compare your logo and slogan with another group.

Challenge 8B

Task 1

Student B

Work with Students A and C to design a corporate image, including a logo and slogan for a clothing company. Use the following notes which you made while interviewing the Personnel Manager.

* image should be of a company that takes care of and looks after its workers.
* need to develop a "green" image using natural fibers and environmentally-friendly materials
* best place to advertise would be in young people's magazines

Task 2

Compare your logo and slogan with another group.

Challenge 9

Task 1

a **Group Work** Look again at the various tasks in Chain 1 on pages 68–69. Each group should select a different cause and prepare a plan to support it. Decide how to raise money and think about other kinds of volunteer support that you might get.

b **Group Work** Decide what you would say to get the different kinds of support. Prepare a group presentation.

Task 2

a **Group Work** Class presentation. Take turns presenting your cause to the rest of the class.

b **Group Work** Now vote on which cause to support.

Challenge 11A

Task 1

With the information you have available, decide which of these people would be the best to . . .

- work with ....
- prepare for an exam with ....
- hang out with ....
- have around in an emergency ....

NAME	AT WORK	AT HOME	AT PLAY
Maurice	always in a hurry to get things done; gets upset when things go wrong	?	loves to play sports and competitive games; gets upset when he loses
Kim	?	doesn't mind a messy place as long as it's clean	?
Jodie	doesn't mind when things go wrong; is the first to take a coffee break	?	great conversationalist; enjoys physical team sports but is not very good at board games
Kerry	?	likes to organize others	?

Task 2

a Ask your partner questions about the behavior of these people and complete the missing parts of the chart.

b Now work with your partner to decide who would be the best person . . .

- to work with ....
- to prepare for an exam with ....
- to hang out with ....
- to have around in an emergency ....

my name is   exercise!
hello
how are you?   where do you live?   my sister

Challenge 8C

* image should be of a dynamic young company that is developing rapidly
* need to develop a product range to appeal to fashionable young people in their twenties
* need smart, casual line of clothes for people with a limited budget
* advertising campaign should be on TV using rock music video-clip format

Task 1

Student C

Work with Students A and B to design a corporate image, including a logo and slogan for a clothing company. Use the following notes which you made while interviewing the Advertising Manager.

Task 2

When you have finished, compare your logo and slogan with another group.

Challenge 15A

Who is the most optimistic? Who is the most pessimistic? Report to your partners what Susan says, and decide.

66 I think that childhood was the best time in my life, so I guess in some ways I'm a little more backward-looking than many people. On the other hand, I don't believe that the environment has deteriorated as much as the media suggests. I don't think that I'll be better off as I get older, either. And I don't think I'm as well off as my parents were at my age. 99

Challenge 11B

Task 1

With the information you have available, decide which of these people would be the best person to . . .

- work with ....
- prepare for an exam with ....
- hang out with ....
- have around in an emergency ....

NAME	AT WORK	AT HOME	AT PLAY
Maurice	?	often takes work home so has little time for family and friends	?
Kim	often arrives late for work; enjoys the routine of work but does not like new challenges	?	is good at introducing people to each other; a good mixer and sympathetic listener
Jodie	?	likes to take frequent vacations so is not often at home	?
Kerry	is constantly applying for new jobs; usually tries to do several things at once	?	talks about self a lot but is amusing company at parties; likes to win at games

Task 2

a Ask your partner questions about the behavior of these people and complete the missing parts of the chart.

b Now work with your partner to decide who would be the best person . . .

- to work with ....
- to prepare for an exam with ....
- to hang out with ....
- to have around in an emergency ....

Challenge 12A

Task 1

Student A

You are trapped in a remote place with the following people. Here is what other people said about them. Which one will you elect as your leader? Work with Student B to make notes on each person and then decide.

Graciela's boss: "I don't have too many complaints about Graciela. She's independent—in fact she's a bit of a loner. She also tends not to listen to others."

Conrad's coworker: "The good thing about working with Conrad is that he gets things done. He's really self-motivated."

Steve's housemate: "I used to share an apartment with Steve, but I moved out because he was always criticizing the others in the apartment. Also, he'd get angry if we had to decide on something, and the decision didn't go his way—you know, he's one of those guys who always has to get his own way."

Rebecca's teacher: "Rebecca was one of my favorite students. She is a very persistent person—never gives up. She was also very good at getting others involved in things."

	POSITIVE	NEGATIVE
Graciela		
Conrad		
Stephen		
Rebecca		

Task 2

Now compare your choice with another pair.

where you're invited... go to the movies! meet me for lunc
what do you do why
is my family neighborhood

Challenge 15B

Who is the most optimistic? Who is the most pessimistic? Report to your partners what George says, and decide.

66 I have a good life, and I expect to be better off as I get older. I'm certainly better off financially than I was when I was in my twenties. On the other hand, I don't think that my children will be as well off as I am. I think that there will be fewer educational and employment opportunities and with all the environmental problems we are facing, I don't think that the world will be as pleasant a place to live. Unfortunately, science doesn't seem to be able to provide solutions to major problems such as AIDS, and environmental problems. 99

Task 1

Student B

You are trapped in a remote place with the following people. Here is what other people said about them. Which one will you elect as your leader? Work with Student A to make notes on each person and then decide.

Graciela's coworker: "I don't mind working with her at all. Graciela has a very strong personality, which might put some people off, but I think it's a positive thing. She's also good at communicating her ideas."

Conrad's boss: "I had to move Conrad to another part of the firm. He wasn't good at getting others to do things, and would tend to do them himself rather than getting the cooperation of the people he was working with."

Steve's teacher: "I always knew that Steve would become an artist or a designer. In school, he always had very creative ideas, and came up with interesting solutions to problems."

Rebecca's ex-boyfriend: "I guess we split up because our personalities are so different. I'm easygoing, very laid back. Rebecca's the driven type. She was always getting impatient when people didn't understand what she was talking about."

	POSITIVE	NEGATIVE
Graciela		
Conrad		
Stephen		
Rebecca		

Task 2

Now compare your choice with another pair.

Challenge 14 A

Task 1

Brainstorm. Think of up to five arguments *in favor of* the following statement: "Young people who paint graffiti on other people's property are destructive vandals who ought to be punished."

1 ....

2 ....

3 ....

4 ....

5 ....

Task 2

a Select three or four people to speak against the following statement: "Young people who paint graffiti on other people's property are destructive vandals who ought to be punished."

b The speakers take ten minutes to prepare their arguments and decide who is to say what.

c The rest of the group make a checklist of points for and against the statement.

Task 3

a Each speaker has three minutes to state his/her case. Alternate between those speaking for and against.

b As they speak, the rest of the class uses the checklist developed in Task 2 to evaluate which points have been covered.

Task 4

The class votes on which side presented the best case.

Challenge 13

Task 1

Study the following events and put them in order (1 to 14).

.... While Jack was in the store, his car was towed away.

.... When he got to her house, he found that he didn't have enough money to pay for the taxi.

.... She said that she'd never forget her birthday.

.... She'd been waiting over two hours when he finally arrived.

.... He was supposed to have arrived at seven, but didn't get there till after 9:30.

.... She said that she didn't believe him, because she'd called his office and no one had answered.

.... Jack had to ask his girlfriend for a loan.

.... He tried to take a bus, but they were all full.

.... He parked in a no parking zone.

.... Jack decided to drive to his girlfriend's place to take her out for her birthday.

.... In the end, he had to take a taxi.

.... He stopped on the way to buy her some flowers.

.... She was very angry and upset.

.... He lied and said that he'd been delayed at work by the boss, because he was embarrassed about the car being towed.

Task 2

Make up an ending to the story and tell it to another group.

Challenge 14B

Task 1

Brainstorm. Think of up to five arguments *in favor of* the following statement: "Young people who paint murals on public property are creative artists who ought to be rewarded."

1 ....

2 ....

3 ....

4 ....

5 ....

Task 2

a Select three or four people to speak against the following statement: "Young people who paint murals on public property are creative artists who ought to be rewarded."

b The speakers take ten minutes to prepare their arguments and decide who is to say what.

c The rest of the group make a checklist of points for and against the statement.

Task 3

a Each speaker has three minutes to state his/her case. Alternate between those speaking for and against.

b As they speak, the rest of the class uses the checklist developed in Task 2 to evaluate which points have been covered.

Task 4

The class votes on which side presented the best case.

Challenge 15C

Who is the most optimistic? Who is the most pessimistic? Report to your partners what Yvonne says, and decide.

66 I'll be fifty-five next birthday, and so I've seen a lot of changes taking place. I've seen the world come to the brink of nuclear war. I've seen footage of famine in Africa. But for me, life keeps getting better and better. I'm certainly a lot better off than I was when I was young, and I'm better off than my parents were when they were in their fifties. I think that science has the potential to solve the problems we face. 99

Grammar Summaries

Unit 1

1 Prepositional phrases

We lived *on the floor* above the noisiest people on the block.
It was pointless trying to sleep *during the festival*.
We waited *for hours* but he never came back.
They went *into the bus station* when the storm started.
They waited *in the bus station* until the storm passed.
Holding the party *on a boat* was a stroke of genius.
Getting *into the program* was a real challenge.
Unfortunately, the joke went *over their heads*.
I haven't been back there *since they threw me out*.
We went *to the jazz festival* together last year.
They came *towards us* looking threatening.
I walked *under the ladder* to show I wasn't superstitious.
I trained *until eight o'clock*.

2 Modals: *can/could/would/would mind*

Can you make it to the party?	Yes, I can.	No, I can't.
Could you invite Mike as well?	Yes, I could.	No, I couldn't.
Would you be able to come at around eight?	Yes, I would.	No, I wouldn't.
Would they mind if I brought a friend?	Yes, they would.	No, they wouldn't.

Unit 2

1 Short responses

A: Are you still reading that awful horoscope column in the newspaper?
B: Not since it said I'd win a million dollars.

A: Did you know that I saw a ghost once when I was a kid?
B: I find that hard to believe.

A: Have you seen the guy on TV who can bend spoons by looking at them?
B: No, not yet.

2 Relative adverbials: *where/when/why/how*

I don't really understand how it happened.
The place where it happened was about 50 kilometers from shore.
It was around 5 A.M. when I saw the lights of a tanker coming towards me.
The reason why they didn't see me was because of the huge waves.

Unit 3

1 Present perfect & simple past

Present perfect:
A state continuing from past to present
How long have you been here?
The store has been closed for hours.

Events in a time period leading up to the present
Have you seen the new movie at the Odeon?
I've decided I'm not the party type.

Past tense:
Habits or recurring events
Have you danced with him often?
I've been to ten parties in the last month.

Completed events at a definite time in the past
Did you go to the office party on Friday?
She didn't come to the party because she was sick.

2 Emphasis with *it* & *what*

What I love about my country is the political freedom.
It's the political freedom that I love about my country.
What annoys me about my job is having to work weekends.
It's having to work weekends that annoys me about my job.
What I admire about you is your patience.
It's your patience that I admire about you.

Unit 4

1 *When* & *if* clauses + modals *should/shouldn't*

What should I do if my co-workers smoke in the non-smoking areas at work?
If they smoke in the non-smoking areas, you shouldn't let them get away with it.
If they smoke in the non-smoking areas, you should ask them to stop.

What should I do when my brother comes in late and puts on loud music?
When he puts on loud music, you shouldn't just put up with it, you should ask him to turn it down.

2 Relative clauses with *whose/who/who is*

A: Would you like to share an apartment with someone who smokes?
B: I'd hate to share an apartment with someone who smokes.

A: Would you like to share a house with someone whose friends are always calling?
B: Sharing a house with someone whose friends are always calling wouldn't bother me at all, actually.

A: Would you like to live with someone who's extremely neat?
B: I couldn't stand living with someone who's extremely neat, because it would make me look like a slob.

Unit 6

1 Passives: past and perfect forms

A: When was that famous photo taken?
B: I think it was taken in the thirties. It's been around for many years.

A: Why was the exhibition cancelled?
B: There wasn't enough interest in the subject.

A: How were the pictures arranged?
B: They were put in chronological order—you know, by the year in which they were painted.

2 Reported speech

"Do you want these drinks?" → She asked if we wanted those drinks.
"I put the book right here." → He said that he had put the book right there.
"We wanted to meet you yesterday." → Tony said that he had wanted to meet us the day before.
"I told you about the exam two days ago." → She said that she had told us about the exam two days earlier.

Unit 7

1 Relative clauses with *that* & *whose*

Reptiles are animals that have cold blood.
Reptiles are animals whose blood is cold.

Mammals are animals that have warm blood.
Mammals are animals whose blood is warm.

2 Superlative adjectives with present perfect

Who's the most interesting person you've ever met? → Your brother, actually.
What's the most unusual thing you've ever done? → Hang gliding in California.
What's the most frightening experience you've ever had? → Hang gliding in California.
Where's the most interesting place you've ever visited? → Oh, New York, without a doubt.
Why was the trip to Brazil so memorable? → I made some fantastic friends.

Unit 8

1 Phrasal verbs + gerunds

Tracy's *looking forward to starting* the new job.
We'll have to *cut down on calling* your folks on the West Coast.
The boss decided not to *go through with firing* the front office guy.
Nina *put off telling* Jose she doesn't want to see him any more.
I intend to *keep on asking* her until she says "yes".
You should *cut down on going out* at night until after exams.
I'm not going to *put off telling* him what I think any longer.
They *plan on going* to Seoul for Chinese New Year.
I can't *put up with listening* to your complaints any longer.

2 Indirect questions & requests

Could you help us move the furniture? → I wonder if you could help us move the furniture.
Will it make a difference if we leave? → Do you think it will make a difference if we leave?
Does the new computer system get installed next week? → Can you tell me if the new computer system gets installed next week?
Could they borrow your car? → They wanted to know if they could borrow your car.
What is the teacher planning for us next week? → Can you tell me what the teacher is planning for us next week?

Unit 9

1 Object + infinitive

We want you to read the pamphlet carefully.
They'd like you to call them as soon as possible.
Tracy wants us to sign a petition on human rights.
I'd like you to get some information on Greenpeace for me.
Rebecca wants us to come over on Tuesday night.
Our class wants the whole school to contribute to the appeal.

2 Past conditional

If Winston hadn't become a volunteer aid worker, he wouldn't have gotten to Africa.
We'd never have raised the money if we hadn't all cooperated.
If my sister hadn't become a teacher, she would probably have become a social worker.
If the volunteer worker had been a bit more polite, I might have donated some money.
You wouldn't have gotten the job if you hadn't given that brilliant interview.
I'd have made an official complaint if it had been me who'd been fired.

Unit 11

1   *Wh-* questions + gerund/infinitive

How did you avoid going to the party last night?
What do you expect to do when you graduate?
Where do you hope to live when you return to Brazil?
Who would you consider asking to the party?
What do you intend to do over the weekend?
Why do you dislike watching sports on TV?
What kind of music do you enjoy listening to most?
Why did you deny going to the disco last night?
Why did she refuse to answer our questions?
Why do you want to go to the movies?
What did they suggest buying for the party?

2   Comparatives/superlative + gerund/infinitive

Growing up in the sixties was better than growing up in the seventies.
The best thing about being a child was not having to work.
Being an adult is much more interesting than being a child.
Living in a large city was more stressful than living in a small one.
Learning another language was the most difficult thing I've ever done.

Unit 12

1   Future perfect

I think that by the end of the century, the world population will have doubled.
Do you think that the economy will have improved by the end of the year?
This time next week, we'll have been here for over a year.
By tonight, I'll have spent over eight hours doing my assignment.
Paul thinks that by the end of the year he will have lost his job again.

2   Tag questions

They should have arrived by now, shouldn't they?
You weren't particularly interested in the position, were you?
Maria's been an organizer before, hasn't she?
We shouldn't spend too much time preparing for the interview, should we?
Most of the members of the class are hard-working, aren't they?
I wasn't that late, was I?

Unit 13

1 Review of past & perfect tenses

Simple past
Who lost their job last week?
Rick lost his job.
Susan didn't lose her job.

Present perfect
What's happened to you since we last met?
I've lost my job again.
They haven't found work since moving from the States.

Past perfect
Had you heard about the job before you read the ad?
I'd been in the job a week before anyone spoke to me.
We hadn't been there long before an argument broke out.

Present perfect progressive
Have you been waiting long?
I've been working for Langmore and Johns for three years.
We haven't been getting along lately.

Past progressive
Were you working for the Governor during his election campaign?
I was sitting at my desk when the boss came by and said he wanted to see me.
They weren't waiting for me when I stopped by to pick them up, so I drove on.

2 Supposed to have

A: Who was Adriana supposed to have called last night?
B: She was supposed to have called her parents, but she forgot.
A: What is something you are supposed to do by the end of the month?
B: I'm supposed to enroll for a computer course by Friday.

Unit 14

1 Complex passives

In many societies, it is considered bad taste to talk about money and wealth.
In other societies it is believed unlucky to talk about poverty.
Where I come from, it is thought impolite to ask how old someone is.
In years gone by, it was thought extremely rude to allow children to speak in front of adults.

2 Idioms

Tony thinks that most politicians are a lot of hot air.
I'm having second thoughts about buying a car since the cost of gas went up.
Tracy's really indiscrete—she's always putting her foot in her mouth.
I'm looking for another job because my boss is always throwing his weight around.
It doesn't help to be told to snap out of it when you're depressed about something.
Everyone in the new class is hitting it off so well that we decided to have a party.
I had to bite my tongue so I didn't insult your friend the other night when he was rude to me.
If the boss spoke to me like that, I'd give her a piece of my mind.

Photographs

Cover Sextant, Courtesy Peabody Essex Museum, Salem, MA. Photo by Mark Sexton; All maps Canada/Rand McNally © Repolgle Globes; **9** © Superstock (c); © Randall Hyman/Stock Boston (bl) © Superstock (bc); © Keren Su/Stock Boston (br); © Jay Freis/The Image Bank (t); © Alan Becker/The Image Bank; (tl) **13** © Richard Pasley/Stock Boston; © Jonathan Stark/Heinle & Heinle Publishers (all others); **15** © JS/H&H; **17** © JS/H&H (r, br, bl); © Hans Wendler/The Image Bank (t); Illustrations from The Rider-Waite® Tarot Deck reproduced by permission of U.S. Games Systems, Inc., Stamford, CT 06902 USA. Copyright © 1971 by U.S. Games Systems, Inc. Further reproduction prohibited. The Rider-Waite® Tarot Deck is a registered trademark of U.S. Games Systems, Inc. (tl); © Jay Freis/The Image Bank; **20** © JS/H&H; **25** © Churchill & Klehr/Tony Stone Images, Inc. (l); © Dennis O'Clair/Tony Stone Images, Inc. (r); © Claude Charlier/The Stock Market (bl); © David Nausbaum/ Tony Stone Images, Inc. (bcl); Catalyst/The Stock Market (bcr); © JS/H&H (br); Courtesy of Image Club/1-800-661-9410 (t); © Michael Melford/The Image Bank(tl); **26** © UPI/ Bettman; **28** © Superstock; **29** © JS/H&H (all); **31** © Stuart Cohen/Comstock **33** © JS/H&H (c, bl, bc, br);Courtesy of Image Club/1-800-661-9410 (t) **36** © JS/H&H; **39** © Bob Daemmrich/Stock Boston; **41** © JS/H&H (lc, ltc, lbc, lb); PhotoDisc ((t); © Garry Gay/The Image Bank (tl) **43** Joan Miró, *Head of a Catalan Peasant*, 1924–25. Oil. Courtesy of the Granger Collection. **44** © John Colletti/Stock Boston (t)); © JS/H&H (all others); **47** © JS/H&H (all); **51** © Superstock (l); © John Cancalosi/Stock Boston (c); © Comstock (bl); © JS/H&H (bcr); © Tom McCarthy/PhotoEdit (br); © Don Klumpp/The Image Bank (t); © James Carmichael/The Image Bank (tl); **53** © Russ Kinne/ Photo Researchers; **55** © Comstock (tl); © Townsend P. Dickinson/Comstock (tr); © JS/H&H (bl); © Super- stock (br); **57** © Comstock; **59** © JS/H&H (all); © Frank Whitney/The Image Bank(t): **60** © JS/H&H; **62** © JS/H&H; **65** © JS/H&H; **67** © Anna E. Zuckerman/PhotoEdit (l); © Oxfam Hong Kong (r); © JS/H&H (bl); © Brent Jones/Stock Boston (br); Courtesy Project Bread, Boston, MA (t, tl); **68** Courtesy The French Library and Cultural Center, Inc., Boston, MA (cr); © JS/H&H (all others); **70** © Peter Erbland/ Aids Action Committee of Massachusetts, Inc.; **73** © Comstock; **75** © David Sailors/The Stock Market (l); © Superstock (r); © JS/H&H (bl); © Jon Feinghersh/ The Stock Market (br); PhotoDisc (t); © Garry Gay/ The Image Bank (tl) **77** © Comstock (r); © JS/H&H (all others); © Pat Lacroix/The Image Bank (t); **78** © JS/H&H; **80** © JS/H&H; **81** © Linder Elem/Stock Boston; **82** UPI/Bettman **83** © JS/H&H; **85** © Charles Gupton/The Stock Market(l); © Stacy Pickerell/Tony Stone Images, Inc. (r); © JS/H&H (bl); © Laura Elliott/Comstock (br); **86** © JS/H&H (all); **87** Lisa de George; **89** © Bob Daemmrich/Stock Boston; **93** © Jo Van Os/The Image Bank (t); © James H. Carmichael, Jr./The Image Bank **94** © The Granger Collection (l); © UPI/Bettman (c); © Bob Daemmrich/Stock Boston (r); **98** © JS/H&H; **101** © Superstock (l); © JS/H&H (all others); © Gary S. Chapman/The Image Bank (t); © Lisa de George (tl); **105** © JS/H&H; **120** © JS/H&H; **122** © JS/H&H (all); **123** © JS/H&H; **124** © JS/H&H (all); **128** © JS/H&H

Illustrations

63 Lisa de George; **All others** Kevin Spaulding

Text

11 From Dragon Boat Festival brochure, courtesy of the Hong Kong Tourist Association. **19** From *Literary Outlaw: The Life and Times of William S. Burroughs* by T. Morgan. Copyright © 1991 by T. Morgan. Published by Pimlico/Random House. **22** From "Miracle Skipper Survives" by Rebecca Lang from *The Canberra Times*, December 29, 1993. Copyright © 1993 by *The Canberra Times*. **26** From "United States of America," p. 1248 of the *Cambridge Encyclopedia*. Copyright © 1990 by Cambridge University Press. Reprinted by permission. **35** From "You Can Get a Good Night's Rest" by Barbara Floria from *Vitality*, August 1994. Copyright © 1994 by *Vitality*. Reprinted by permission. **60** The Boston Phone Directory, p. 19. Copyright © 1995 NYNEX Information Resources Company. Reprinted by permission of NYNEX Information Resources Company. **68** Adapted from Oxfam. Advertisement used courtesy of Oxfam Hong Kong. **82** From "Tinker, Tailor, Paleontologist or Hairdresser?" by Deborah Holder, *The Independent on Sunday,* April 10, 1994. Copyright © 1994 by Newspaper Publishing PLC, London. Reprinted by permission. **86** From "Voices Across America" in USA Today, July 13, 1993. Copyright © 1993 by the Roper Center for Public Opinion Research. Reprinted by permission. **97** From "The Same Old Life" by Kenneth A. Walston from *Vitality,* June 1994. Copyright © 1994 by *Vitality*. Reprinted by permission.

Irregular Verb Chart

SIMPLE FORM ►	PAST FORM ►	PAST PARTICIPLE
arise	arose	arisen
be	was	been
begin	began	begun
bite	bit	bitten
blow	blew	blown
break	broke	broken
bring	brought	brought
build	built	built
buy	bought	bought
catch	caught	caught
choose	chose	chosen
cost	cost	cost
cut	cut	cut
do	did	done
draw	drew	drawn
drink	drank	drunk
drive	drove	driven
eat	ate	eaten
fall	fell	fallen
feed	fed	fed
feel	felt	felt
fight	fought	fought
find	found	found
fly	flew	flown
forget	forgot	forgotten
get	got	gotten
give	gave	given
go	went	gone
grow	grew	grown
have	had	had
hear	heard	heard
hold	held	held
keep	kept	kept
know	knew	known
learn	learned	learned
leave	left	left

SIMPLE FORM ►	PAST FORM ►	PAST PARTICIPLE
let	let	let
light	lit	lit
lose	lost	lost
make	made	made
mean	meant	meant
meet	met	met
pay	paid	paid
put	put	put
read	read	read
ride	rode	ridden
ring	rang	rung
run	ran	run
say	said	said
see	saw	seen
sell	sold	sold
send	sent	sent
shoot	shot	shot
show	showed	shown
shut	shut	shut
sing	sang	sung
sink	sank	sunk
sit	sat	sat
sleep	slept	slept
speak	spoke	spoken
stand	stood	stood
swim	swam	swum
take	took	taken
teach	taught	taught
tell	told	told
think	thought	thought
throw	threw	thrown
understand	understood	understood
wake	woke	woken
wear	wore	worn
win	won	won
write	wrote	written